GRAND CANYON
River at Risk

GRAND CANYON
RIVER AT RISK

Wade Davis

Preface by Robert F. Kennedy, Jr. ~ *Foreword by* Greg MacGillivray

Principal photography by Chris Rainier

Additional photography by Wade Davis, MacDuff Everton,
Alan Kozlowski & Michael Nichols

Inspired by MacGillivray Freeman's IMAX® Theatre film
Grand Canyon Adventure: River at Risk

Earth Aware Editions

San Rafael, CA

CONTENTS

The sun rises over the Colorado River, seen from the Toroweap Overlook

Finding Inspiration in the Grand Canyon

Greg MacGillivray

IF YOU'VE STOOD ON THE RIM OF THE GRAND CANYON OR BEEN FORTUNATE ENOUGH TO RAFT DOWN THE MIGHTY COLORADO RIVER THAT CARVED THIS GREAT PLACE, YOU HAVE MOST CERTAINLY FELT AWED BY THE POWER OF WATER and the beauty it creates. Water is earth's most precious resource and is essential to human life, but the Canyon reminds us that water is an extraordinary force of nature. Of course, water can also be a source of sheer fun.

As a filmmaker who grew up in Southern California with a passion for surfing, I have always been drawn to water. I started my career making surfing films in high school with my buddies. Countless hours spent on my surfboard instilled in me a deep love of the ocean and an appreciation for the power of water to inspire a lifestyle and a mindset in harmony with our liquid planet.

Years later, after becoming captivated by the visually immersive IMAX Theatre film format—with its brilliant, crystal clear images projected onto giant screens eighty feet tall—it occurred to me that I could use this state-of-the-art film format to share my love of water and my concern for the declining health of our waterways. I committed myself to making a series of IMAX Theatre films dedicated to water conservation themes—films such as *The Living Sea*, *Dolphins*, and *Coral Reef Adventure*—that would inspire audiences to fall in love with our world's oceans and be moved enough to take greater steps toward protecting them and nurturing them back to health.

When I first started thinking about making a film about our planet's growing shortage of clean, fresh water, the Colorado River, with its powerful rapids sweeping through the red-rimmed walls of the Grand Canyon, immediately came to mind. Here, I thought, would be the ideal arena for creating a truly visceral IMAX 3D experience while challenging the audience to think seriously about water conservation. The Colorado is one of the most iconic yet over-allocated rivers in the world. In our film *Grand Canyon Adventure: River at Risk*, it becomes a metaphor for what's happening to rivers all over the world.

To give voice to the urgency of the water crisis, I turned to two high-powered, Harvard-educated thinkers—two men with a lifetime dedication to water conservation. I had heard about Wade Davis, a brilliant anthropologist, outdoorsman, author, and lecturer, whose studies of river cultures around the world have become bestselling books. At the same time I was also learning about Robert F. Kennedy, Jr.'s campaigns to save rivers from polluters. Kennedy is a living hero to many people and *Time* magazine called him a "Hero for the Planet." He is perhaps best known for his work saving the Hudson River.

It wasn't until I talked to them, though, that I realized that not only do they share the same global environmental mission, they also have similarly aged teenage daughters, Kick Kennedy and Tara Davis, who were each on the eve of going away to college. I immediately became enamored with the idea of bringing these two families together, of inviting audiences to experience the Colorado River through their eyes. I imagined a kind of last-hurrah trip with two fathers about to send their daughters off to start their own independent journeys—and with that came a beautiful sense of each father passing on to his daughter the torch of these important battles for the environment.

Our time together on the river was one of those amazing life experiences where you're transported out of your daily

I**F THERE IS MAGIC ON THIS PLANET,**
IT IS CONTAINED IN WATER.
—L**OREN** E**ISELEY**

routine and inspired to see the world in new ways. I'll never forget sitting around the campfire listening to Bobby talk passionately about wilderness and the natural right of all humankind to clean, safe water. Bobby is a powerful communicator, and we were all deeply moved by his eloquent and fiery call-to-action. Wade's stories about remote river cultures that are spiritually connected to their local waterways were equally inspiring. How can it be that as Westerners, we have become so psychically removed from the water that sustains us?

As we journeyed down the river together, making the movie and having fun, I was also impressed by how these men's remarkable daughters have internalized the messages they have heard from birth—messages about the importance of conservation. Hearing them speak of their own ambitions and strategies for making a difference gave me great hope that the next generation will be able to meet the challenges passed on to them from my own generation.

The water problem is serious and complex, and it's going to take big solutions to get things back into balance again. But people have an amazing ability to come up with innovative solutions to life's big challenges. It's not going to be easy, but even if we alter our behavior just a little, we can make a huge difference.

Deep in the canyon, when all is still, hope abounds.

✵ We live on a water planet. Two atoms of hydrogen bonded to an atom of oxygen, multiplied by the miracles of physics and chemistry, are transformed into clouds, rivers, and rain. Pour the contents of all the lakes and oceans, the snowfields and inland seas, the underground aquifers and the Antarctic ice, into a vessel and it would contain 1.4 billion cubic kilometers of water. Unfortunately, most of it would be too saline to drink, and of the 2.5 percent that is fresh, more than two-thirds is, at least for the moment, locked away in ice or trapped underground in the pores of sedimentary rocks.

The water we need, the clear taste of life, is found only in our lakes, which, more often than not, are the source of our rivers, and these together contain only one quarter of 1 percent of the world's freshwater. If all the water on Earth could be stored in a five-liter container, what is available to us to drink would scarcely fill a teaspoon. Of this precious fluid, we squander fully 80 percent on industrial irrigation, a euphemistic term that implies the attempt to grow specific crops in places where such plants were never meant to be. ✵

The water sinks low at Lake Powell

PREFACE

Robert F. Kennedy, Jr.

 IN 1967 MY FATHER TOOK ME AND EIGHT OF MY BROTHERS AND SISTERS ON A COLORADO RIVER WHITEWATER TRIP THROUGH THE GRAND CANYON. JUST ABOVE OUR PUT-IN STOOD THE GLEN CANYON DAM, WHICH HAD BEEN completed three years before; Lake Powell was still filling. The new dam complemented the Hoover Dam, nearly three hundred miles downstream at the other end of the Grand Canyon. Together they promised to irrigate a thirsty West, generate hydropower, and create great lakes with recreational opportunities for millions. But critics thought the Glen Canyon Dam a wasteful and reckless boondoggle to corporate agriculture and greedy developers. Environmentalists said the dam would destroy the Grand Canyon National Park's unique ecology and that the lakes would lose horrendous amounts of water to evaporation and seepage and would soon fill with sediment.

That year we camped on the Colorado's massive sandbars and bathed and swam in her warm seventy-degree water and caught some native fish from its abundant schools. In 2006, I returned to paddle the Grand Canyon with my daughter Kick and my life-long hero and Harvard classmate (we sat through anthropology class together) Wade Davis—the real-life Indiana Jones—and his beautiful daughter Tara, with whom Kick formed the kind of strong bonds that occur so often during whitewater adventures. We embarked as guests of another of my icons, Greg MacGillivray, the world's foremost IMAX cinematographer. I was sad to see that the spacious sandy beaches and massive driftwood piles where I had camped with my father were gone, the sands that once fed them trapped above the dam.

The river, which should be warm and muddy, is clear and a frigid forty-six degrees. Four of her eight native fish species are extinct, with two others headed there soon. The canyon's beaver, otter, and muskrat populations have also disappeared, as have its indigenous insect species. Sediment has already flatlined hydropower and nearly choked the upper reaches of Lake Powell, which is in severe decline as a tourist destination. The Colorado River no longer reaches the sea or feeds the great estuaries in the Gulf of California that once teemed with life. Instead, it ignominiously dies in the Sonoran desert. What was once a dynamic and specialized ecosystem cutting through the greatest monument to America's national heritage has been transformed into a cold-water plumbing conduit between the two largest reservoirs in

Left to Right: *Robert F. Kennedy, Jr., Kick Kennedy, Tara Davis, and Wade Davis*

the United States—monuments to greed, shortsightedness, and corporate power.

And all the gravest prophecies of the scientists and environmentalists have come true. The reservoirs are emptying due to human consumption and evaporation, a situation now exacerbated by climate change. Lake Powell is now nearly a hundred feet below its capacity level. Hydropower revenues for repayment to the U.S. Treasury have been at a standstill for six years. Recreation access at the upper reaches of Lake Mead and Lake Powell are now obstructed by savannahs of sedimentary mud. Water quality is dropping precipitously and farmers need more water to flush the dissolved solids from their fields. Sprawl development and agribusiness consumption triggered by the dam's original promise continue their ferocious pace.

The Colorado River has nothing more to give and a train wreck is imminent. But while scientists continue to sound the warning, the river managers insist on business as usual, encouraging wasteful agricultural uses, the proliferation of urban sprawl, and dramatic increases in consumption. They have engineered a system geared to reward the powerful, destroy the river, and impoverish the rest of us.

The Colorado River is the poster child for bad river management hijacked by the water and power agencies who obstruct and control her waters to favor hydropower production over managing the river as a national park. The federal government provides oceans of money to corporate agribusiness to raise wasteful water-dependent crops like rice and alfalfa in the desert. Meanwhile, local and state governments encourage sprawling and water-hungry commercial and residential developments by offering tax breaks and by subsidizing harmful infrastructure such as roads, sewer lines, and electricity. With such inducements developers are building golf courses and swimming pools in the Arizona desert. They have drained the Colorado River dry and are now depleting the 112-million-acre, ten-million-year-old Ogallala Aquifer under the Great Plains states, which has dropped several hundred feet since modern irrigation practices surged following World War II.

It's not too late to implement rational water policy in the West that would serve America's citizens rather than the greedy, powerful few and that would create an example for the democratic use of public-trust resources worldwide. If the grotesque handouts ceased, we could easily meet today's needs, while protecting the rights of our children. In order to succeed we must adopt healthy legal and economic rules that reward the efficient use of resources and punish their inefficient use. Our legal system must confront polluters with the social costs of their activities.

But first, Americans need to be aware of their rights and the jeopardy those rights face before the juggernaut of corporate power. Democracy affirms individual rights to our natural resources. But those rights cannot survive without a courageous citizenry that insists that their government not merely cater to commerce and industry but that it aggressively protects its citizenry's right to good health; safe air, water, and food; and the enrichment of America's national heritage and God's creation.

The struggle for control of water is intertwined with the fight to preserve democracy from the corrosive impacts of expanding corporate power. The best measure of how a democracy functions is how it distributes the goods of the land; the air, waters, wandering animals, fisheries, and public lands, otherwise known as the "public trust," or the "commons." By their nature these resources cannot be reduced to private property but are the shared assets of all the people held in trust for future generations.

Since ancient times, the laws of all just and equitable nations have protected these public trust assets as the property of all citizens, be they humble or noble, rich or poor. Roman law, our most ancient legal heritage, held that the most fundamental "natural," or God-given, law required that the "air, running water, the sea, and consequently the sea shore" could not be owned as private property but were "common to all" Roman citizens. The Romans vigorously protected the waterways and the resources of the sea, seashore, estuaries, wetlands, and fisheries from control by private individuals. Everyone has the right to use the commons, but only in a way that does not diminish its use by others.

The first acts of a tyranny invariably include efforts to privatize the commons. Despotic governments typically allow favored persons or powerful entities to capture and consolidate the public trust and steal the commonwealth from its citizens.

Following Rome's collapse, Europe's kings and feudal lords appropriated public trust assets, including rivers and streams, and dispensed them without regard to public rights. In the early years of the thirteenth century, Britain's King John

LEAVE IT AS IT IS. THE AGES HAVE BEEN AT WORK ON IT, AND MAN CAN ONLY MAR IT. WHAT YOU CAN DO IS TO KEEP IT FOR YOUR CHILDREN, YOUR CHILDREN'S CHILDREN AND FOR ALL WHO COME AFTER YOU, AS ONE OF THE GREAT SIGHTS WHICH EVERY AMERICAN, IF HE CAN TRAVEL AT ALL, SHOULD SEE.

—THEODORE ROOSEVELT

fenced in England's forests and streams, erected navigational tolls, and placed weirs in the rivers in order to sell private monopolies to the fisheries. The exclusion of the public from the rivers and waterways, and the stifling of commerce that ensued, helped prompt a citizens' revolt. In 1215 angry, armed citizens confronted King John at Runnymede, forcing him to sign the Magna Carta, which laid the foundation for constitutional democracy by guaranteeing the personal liberties of the people of England. Centuries later it served as the blueprint for the Bill of Rights in the U.S. Constitution. Among the rights reaffirmed by the Magna Carta were "liberty of navigation" and a "free fishery" so that, according to Britain's seminal legal authority, Sir William Blackstone, "the rivers that were fenced [by the King] were directed to be laid open." Subsequent court decisions interpreted that document to mean that "the King was trustee" holding public waters "as protector of public and common rights" and that "he could not appropriate them to his own use." Eleventh-century French law provided that "the running water and springs … are not to be held by lords … nor are they to be maintained … in any other way than that their people may always be able to use them." Thirteenth-century Spanish law likewise ensured the public inalienable rights to rivers, springs, and shores.

Neither could the King sell public trust assets to a private party. The nineteenth-century legal scholar Henry Schultes described public trust rights as "unalienable." He explained that "things which relate to the public good cannot be given, sold, or transferred by the King to another person." Henry William Woolrych, another leading legal scholar of the period, added that "notwithstanding such a grant, if the public interest be invaded, or the privileges of the people narrowed, the grant, *pro tanto*, is void."

Following the American Revolution, each state became sovereign, inheriting from King George III the trusteeship of public lands and waters and wildlife within its borders. Both the federal government and the individual states recognized the public trust in their statutes and ordinances. For instance, Massachusetts' "Great Pond Ordinance" of 1641 assured public access to all consequential water bodies, and the federal government's Northwest Ordinance of 1787 gave all U.S. citizens unrestrained access to all the tributaries of the St. Lawrence and the Mississippi and proclaimed that those waters and "the carrying

places between shall be common highways and forever free."

The struggle over the world's water resources will be the defining struggle of the twenty-first century. In 1999, following the advice of the World Bank, the Bolivian government allowed the city of Cochabamba to contract with a subsidiary of the Bechtel Corporation to take over the city's public water supply. The company immediately raised water rates, causing profound hardship for all but the city's wealthiest citizens. The public revolted against the rising rates. Massive street protests pitted rock-throwing mobs of Cochabamba's poor against riot police who killed and maimed them. This mini-revolution caused Bolivia's government to collapse and to rescind the privatization of the city's water. This was no communist mob bent on nationalizing legitimate private property. Cochabamba's citizens were engaged in the most fundamental fight for democratic rights.

Like the citizens of Great Britain in 1215, Cochabamba's citizens saw the privatization of the commons as a threat to their democracy and their lives. While privatization controversies in this country have not yet provoked hot confrontations like Cochabamba's, local public utilities across North America are even now conveying water supplies that have benefited from substantial public investment to private companies, often at fire-sale prices. In recent years, only vigorous protests by citizens have kept corporations from privatizing the water supplies in places like Lexington, Kentucky, and Stockton, California. In the Grand Canyon and elsewhere, a more subtle but equally effective privatization of public trust waters is occurring as governments subsidize reckless and unsustainable water usages that favor avaricious developers, powerful utilities, and agribusiness barons over the American public. Destructive government policies are draining our nation's rivers and aquifers and trampling our democratic rights. It's time for another kind of Battle of Runnymede, a peaceful uprising that will return to Americans their fundamental rights to their waterways.

Redwall Cavern

INTRODUCTION

Wade Davis

I HAVE ALWAYS BEEN DRAWN TO RIVERS. MY HEROES AS A BOY GROWING UP IN QUÉBEC WERE THE *COUREURS DE BOIS*, THE FUR TRADERS AND EXPLORERS WHO BROKE OPEN A CONTINENT. I WOULD SPEND HOURS ON THE BANKS OF THE ST. LAWRENCE, imagining their journeys up the river to the Ottawa, past the islands of Georgian Bay to the Superior lakehead, and beyond to the far reaches of the Athabaska territory, through the lands of Huron and Cree, Blackfoot and Kaska, to the mountains of Caledonia and the Pacific shore.

The year I became the father of a little girl we named Tara, I bought a modest lodge in the Stikine Valley of British Columbia, some nine hundred miles north of Vancouver. From our dock we look east to the Sacred Headwaters, a rugged knot of mountains where by a remarkable accident of geography are born three of Canada's most important salmon rivers, the Skeena, Nass, and Stikine. When John Muir saw but the lower third of the Stikine River in 1879, he called it a Yosemite 150 miles long. He counted three hundred glaciers and ice fields along its tortured course, and even decided to name his beloved dog after the river. The midsection of the Stikine, which Muir did not see, is the largest and most formidable canyon in Canada, a stretch of furious whitewater that fewer than fifty kayakers have traversed. Known as the K2 of river challenges, it has never been successfully descended by raft.

Not long after we purchased our place, I met a group of young adventurers who had come together to form a rafting company dedicated to the conservation and exploration of the wild rivers of northern Canada. In time we became partners in the enterprise and I was formally licensed as a whitewater guide.

As a result Tara and her younger sister, Raina, grew up riding the rivers every summer, on extraordinary journeys through the most remote reaches of the Canadian North. By the time they were young teens they had participated in the first commercial descents of the Sheslay, Taku, Turnagain, Sutlahini, Inklin, Nakina, and Raven's Throat. They knew the Kechika and Liard, the Iskut and Spatsizi, the lower and upper Stikine, and, in a distant departure, had floated the Hulahula from the Brooks Range of Alaska to the Beaufort Sea. All of these rivers run free, as fortunately do most of the waters of northern Canada. In the lower forty-eight, by contrast, there is only a single river, the Yellowstone, which flows for more than five hundred miles uncompromised by dams.

When I, along with Tara, was invited to join a celebration of the Colorado, and travel the length of the Grand Canyon, by reputation the greatest whitewater trip in North America, I was delighted. It was, after all, at Lees Ferry that the modern rafting adventure began. The idea for the expedition originated with Greg MacGillivray, a pioneering IMAX filmmaker and dedicated conservationist. Recognizing that the supply and quality of freshwater was among the most daunting of global environmental challenges, Greg wanted to tell a story of water conservation against the backdrop of the Colorado, at once the most iconic and compromised river in the United States. Inspired no doubt by his love for his own daughter, Meghan, Greg envisioned a journey in which two fathers, each in their own ways advocates for the wild, would run the river with their daughters, just before the girls left home to attend university for the first time.

With this premise in mind Greg recruited the two of us along with Bobby Kennedy, Jr., and his daughter Kick. It was a bold and somewhat risky experiment. The success of the film would in no small measure depend on how these four charac-

Left to Right: *River guide Shana Watahomigie; her daughter Cree Watahomigie; Kick Kennedy and Tara Davis; Robert F. Kennedy, Jr., Greg MacGillivray, and Wade Davis*

ters got along. If the chemistry was not right, it would surely show, especially once projected onto an IMAX Theatre screen six stories tall. As it turned out, any such concerns evaporated within hours of our being on the river. Kick and Tara bonded from the start, forging a friendship that continues to deepen to this day. Bobby and I knew of each other and had met one time before the trip, when by chance we had both addressed a conference on river conservation. But only once we were on the Colorado did we realize the extraordinary ways in which the trajectories of our lives had intersected. We had gone to Harvard at the same time, studied anthropology, and found inspiration in many of the same courses and professors. Both of us had come of age in Colombia, and, as we compared notes, were able to work our way down through the landscape of our memories to countless remote mountain crossroads and small lowland towns that we had both come to know. A single phrase or reference, a forest traversed, a tribe encountered, or an escapade survived, invoked telling laughter that reinforced our growing sense of fraternity even as it left both of our daughters wondering just how crazy their fathers had been in their youth.

Bobby had gone down the Colorado with his father in 1967, a journey that inspired in him a love of whitewater and a passion for rivers that would in time lead him to become the country's foremost advocate of water and river conservation. I found him to be an extraordinary man, charismatic and brash, decent and true, with an irresistible sense of humor and immense reservoirs of physical energy and strength. In one instant he was an Irish bard regaling the guides with some barroom joke. In another he would be orchestrating the entire crew in an impromptu game of football in which the rules changed by the moment, with extra points being awarded on the spot for the most clever and cunning innovation. Kick, running the length of the rafts, bouncing from one pontoon to

the next, catapulting off the rigging of the last to catch a ball in midair instantly turned a touchdown into twenty points. But then, a few minutes later, out on the river, all laughter aside, he would invoke from some deep well of memory a wave of anger and outrage at what had become of his country, offering with the precision of the finest courtroom orator a litany of scandal and betrayal that had left the United States politically, environmentally, and economically weakened and compromised. I had never met a person whose love of country was so sincere and yet so free of chauvinistic cant. When Bobby spoke of his father and his uncles, it was for him a natural thing, a simple invocation of lineage. But for the rest of us, it was as if a magical window had opened onto the past. It left everyone on that river yearning for a time when we might once again have leaders of such caliber.

The opportunity to be with Bobby, Kick, and Tara on the river was a father's dream. I would watch Tara when Bobby spoke of what could be in this country, and see how his words inspired her. She was about to begin college in Colorado. What better way to discover the American Southwest than to know the Grand Canyon and to travel the river with Bobby, with all his hopes and dreams of making this a better world?

One day he told the story of what his father had done when word reached him, in Indianapolis on the campaign trail in 1968, that Martin Luther King, Jr. had been assassinated. Against the advice of those who feared for his safety, he immediately made his way to the inner city, and as a buoyant crowd of thousands grew around him, he climbed onto the flatbed of a truck and in a weary voice announced the tragic and devastating news. As word spread, people fell to the ground, sobbing and reeling with grief. Robert Kennedy struggled momentarily for words, but then, speaking from his heart, he told the crowd quietly that he, too, knew what it meant to lose a brother. To

Twilight at SB Point

Kick Kennedy, Tara Davis, Robert F. Kennedy Jr., and Wade Davis gather around the campfire

a seething assembly of pained and angry men and women, he recited from memory the words of the Greek poet Aeschylus, "In our sleep, pain which cannot forget falls drop by drop upon the heart until, in our own despair, against our will, comes wisdom through the awful grace of God."

What was needed in the United States, Bobby's father went on to say that terrible cold and gray night, was not division and hatred, violence and lawlessness; "but love and wisdom and compassion toward one another, and a feeling of justice toward those who still suffer within our country, whether they be white or black. So I shall ask you tonight to return home, to say a prayer for the family of Martin Luther King, but most importantly to say a prayer for our country, which all of us love—a prayer for understanding and that compassion of which I spoke …. Let us dedicate ourselves to what the Greeks wrote so many years ago: to tame the savageness of man and make gentle the life of this world. Let us dedicate ourselves to that, and say a prayer for our country and our people."

That night, as word of the assassination of Dr. King spread, there were violent riots in 110 American cities. Only Indianapolis, where Bobby's father had spoken, did not burn.

WHEN WE MADE CAMP later that afternoon, Tara came to me, and it seemed like she had become a slightly different person, as if some small part of her innocence had been displaced with a kernel of a greater wisdom. I had seen this one other time, several months before, when she and I had attended a healing ceremony among the Navajo. While I was with the men in the sweat lodge, she had spent the afternoon with a young Cree woman who had come south from Canada to be treated. Together they had walked the desert, and later worked with the women, butchering and preparing the sheep meat for the feast. In the ramshackle trailer camp of the Roadman's family, people kind beyond words, she had been totally at home, hanging out with the women, playing with the kids on the dusty floor. That night as we sat in a circle around the sacred fire in the teepee, the glowing coals spread before the ritual altar in the form of a thunderbird, the young Cree woman, having ingested the sacrament, began to tell the story of her life, a litany of misery that went on for a good two hours, with each anecdote revealing an experience more horrific than the last. All that time Tara sat quietly by her side, the tears flowing like rivers from her eyes.

A S WE ALL GATHERED that first morning at Lees Ferry no one could have known how smoothly things would go. Watching Bobby and Greg speak to the assembled media, with the camera crane rising overhead and the loaded rafts clustered along the shore, I glanced at Kick and Tara, and then to the river, which I viewed with some trepidation. Not for fear of the whitewater, but rather out of concern that this most legendary of river trips might somehow disappoint. Plugged by no fewer than eleven dams, the Colorado is the world's most regulated river. Nearly twenty-five thousand people float down it every year. Its flow is determined not by nature but by technicians responding to the electrical needs of Las Vegas and Phoenix. By the time it reaches the delta its essence has been so drained that there is no water left. It enters the ocean a river only in name.

Hence we embarked on the Colorado exhilarated, but haunted by a question. Could a journey down a river, by any definition plundered and violated, still inspire? What remained to be learned? What lessons might its rocks still tell, its eddies invoke? Could a place where park rangers monitor every broken twig, and where river guides and their clients, out of deference for the many thousands who would follow and camp in the same sands, comb the beaches in search of fragments of food and other microtrash, retain anything of its wild character? If not, what is one to make of this iconic canyon so revered in the American imagination? These were only some of the questions and conceits I carried with me from the landing at Lees Ferry. In the end, of course, the river proved me wrong, making a mockery of my myopic time frame, my parochial concerns. The splendor of the river and its canyon, even today, transcends all that man has done to it.

RIVER NOTES

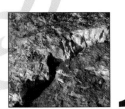 **A** SINGLE FACT OF GEOGRAPHY DEFINES THE AMERICAN WEST. THE CLOUDS THAT SWEEP ACROSS THE PACIFIC BRING RAIN TO THE WESTERN FLANK OF THE SIERRA NEVADA AND DROP as much as 150 inches annually on the forests of the northern Cascades. From the east and south, weather patterns bring moisture from the Atlantic and the Gulf, ensuring that no land receives less than twenty inches of annual precipitation. But travel west of the 100th Meridian, a line of longitude that bisects the Dakotas and Nebraska, running through Dodge City, Kansas, and the dusty back alleys and cattle pens of Abilene, Texas, and you will encounter no place in a thousand miles, from the Mexican frontier in the south to the Canadian border in the north, that receives more than twenty inches of rain in a year. Cities such as Phoenix, Las Vegas, El Paso, and Reno, home to millions, receive less than seven inches annually, as much rain as can fall in Mobile or Miami in a long afternoon.

The entire region, an area the size of Western Europe, was once known as the Great American Desert. But deserts are places of scarcity, minimalist landscapes that, however beautiful, are perceived as being innately hostile, austere, and infertile. Austerity is a notion foreign to the American ethos. Thus, as the frontier moved west, the nomenclature of place shifted, and the desert was transformed in language if not in fact, becoming the Great Basin, the Colorado and Columbia Plateaus, the Snake River Plain, the Blue Mountains, and the Bitterroot Range. But the stark reality remained. The Great Salt Lake, the Black Rock and Painted, the Great Sandy and Death Valley, the Mojave and the Sonoran are all deserts, as dry as many parts of the Sahara. The great cities and scattered towns, the ranches and grim farmsteads, the roadside strip malls, motels, and filling stations, the broken-down drive-ins, and every blue highway pawnshop and plywood souvenir trading post between Taos and Yuma could not exist without the massive manipulation of water.

To engineer this hydrological sleight of hand, there are only two sources—and both are ephemeral. Beneath the ground are vast aquifers, remnants of the Ice Age, finite pools as precious and readily depleted as oil. On the surface, exposed to the relentless sun, are the wild rivers, running like serpents among the ancient rocks and mesas, their flows originating in the snow and ice fields of distant mountains. The largest in terms of volume is the Columbia, which rises in Canada, and its major tributary, the Snake, which is born near the headwaters of the Missouri in the heart of Yellowstone. The longest is the Rio Grande, which runs six hundred miles south from the San Juan Mountains of Colorado along the western flank of the Sangre de Cristo Range, passing through Albuquerque to El Paso, where it turns east and for 1,200 miles forms the international border before reaching the Gulf of Mexico and the Caribbean Sea.

The third of the great rivers is the Colorado, smaller in volume than the Columbia, shorter than the Rio Grande, but surpassing both in its status as the American Nile, the iconic river of the desert West, the muse of poets and songwriters, river guides, shamans, medicine women, eco-warriors, engineers, dam builders, and every farmer from the Grand Valley of Colorado to the Imperial Valley of California. The river provides more than half of the water supply of Los Angeles, San Diego, and Phoenix, and all of the power for Las Vegas, cities that are home to more than twenty-five million people. If the Colorado ceased flowing, the water held in its multiple reservoirs might hold out for three to four years, but after that it would be necessary to abandon most of Southern California and Arizona, and much of Colorado, New Mexico, Utah, and Wyoming. For the entire American Southwest the Colorado is indeed the river of life, which makes it all the more tragic and ironic that by the time it approaches its final destination, it has been reduced to a shadow upon the sand, its delta dry and deserted, its flow a toxic trickle seeping into the sea.

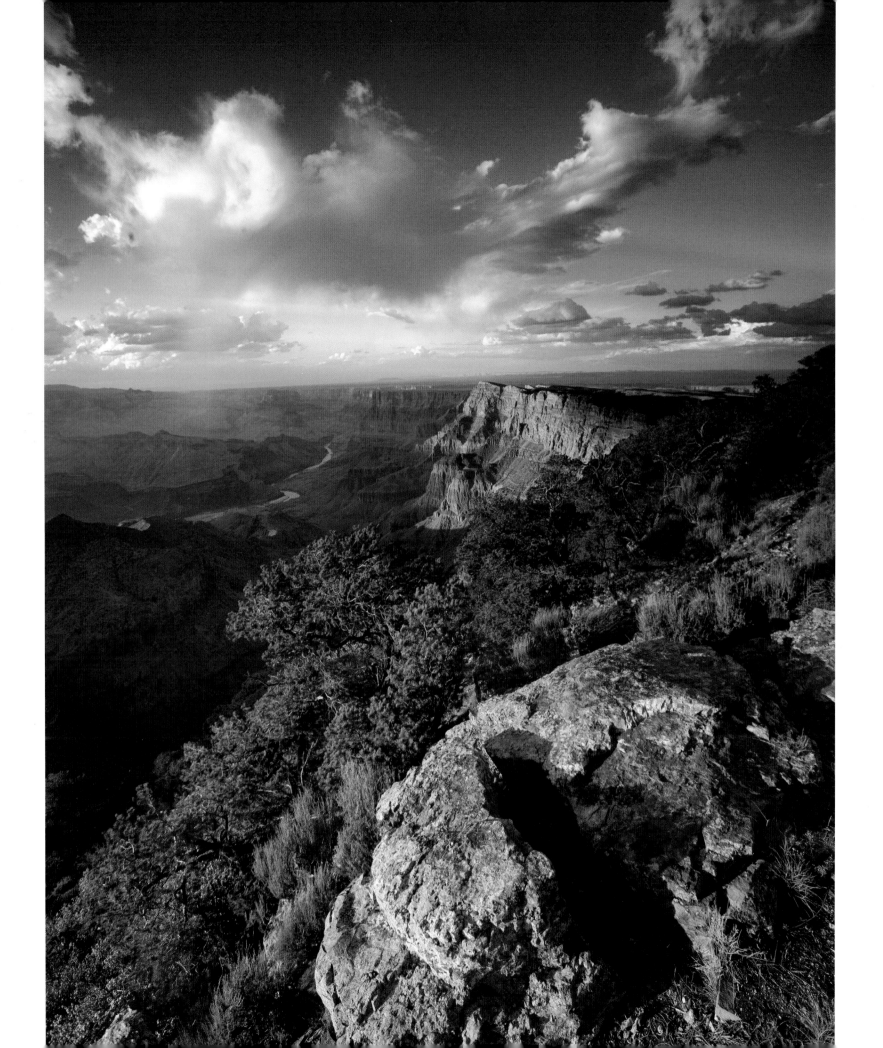

The Colorado River bends dramatically around Point Hansbrough

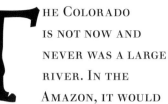

THE COLORADO IS NOT NOW AND NEVER WAS A LARGE RIVER. IN THE AMAZON, IT WOULD SCARCELY RANK AS A SERIOUS TRIBUTARY. DWARFED EVEN WITHIN NORTH AMERICA BY THE MISSOURI and Mississippi, the Yukon, MacKenzie, and St. Lawrence, it is remarkable less for its size than for its setting, the sandstone desert through which it flows. Born of the snowmelt on the west face of Longs Peak just beyond the Continental Divide in Rocky Mountain National Park, the river falls first into a small alpine lake at La Poudre Pass, and then begins a wild ride down the flank of the Cordillera, picking up the runoff of most of western Colorado. Joined by the Eagle and the Roaring Fork, it flattens its trajectory in the Grand Valley, picking up the Gunnison at Grand Junction before moving west into Utah. Running south past Moab and Dead Horse Point, it fuses with the Green, its largest tributary, just above Cataract Canyon, and then flows southwest to be absorbed in a massive reservoir known as Lake Powell. Before the construction of the Glen Canyon Dam the river here ran free for 170 miles through a realm of magic, a canyonland so remote it could be destroyed without notice or attention, and yet so exquisite that its loss would be mourned for generations. Elliot Porter referred to Glen Canyon very simply as "the place that no one knew."

What is remembered of Glen Canyon has been distilled from the notes and letters, the photographs and memories of the very few who had the privilege to experience its wonders and to know the silence of the innumerable stars that once shone upon its depths. Most of what they say is that the river was unexpectedly calm, at least when not in flood. After its tumultuous descent from the snow and ice, a drop of several thousand feet in less than three hundred miles, at Glen Canyon the Colorado entered a place of color and shadow, where red, undulating Navajo Sandstone cliffs enclosed a hidden realm where in the words of a photographer who knew it well, the light itself had a physical, even sensual presence: The deep blue of a spring sky, the emerald green of hanging gardens of ferns and moss, the towering cliffs stained black by rainwater and runoff, the blue glow of moonlight, a thin crescent of night sky over white sandbars of willow and oak. In alcoves and seeps, bank beavers moved among the reeds and deer browsed in the shade of redbud trees. One woke at dawn to the raucous sound of ravens and the singsong music of canyon wrens. And beneath every overhang, up every wash, and in the shadow of cliffs on ground beyond reach of the seasonal floods were to be found not hundreds but thousands of Anasazi remains: ancient granaries and petroglyphs, stairways carved into stone, the remnant walls of house sites and kivas, the patterned outlines of irrigation ditches and channels, all of which disappeared beneath the rising waters when the Glen Canyon Dam closed its floodgates in 1963.

The river running through Glen Canyon and past these exquisite ruins must have been a wild spectacle. Its flow ranged from a summer low of a few thousand cubic feet per second (cfs) to a spring surge of over 300,000 cfs, more than ten times the balanced stream artificially maintained today by the technicians at the spillways. When the summer monsoons broke and the draws and side canyons flashed in flood, these seasonal fluctuations might play out in a single day. The entire canyon would be swept clean to the high-water mark, with vast beaches and boulder fields, formidable rapids, and willowy copses of vegetation simply swallowed in a gargantuan surge of water that was less a river than a slurry carrying an entire desert to the sea. Every year the wild Colorado drew some 200 million tons of silt down its myriad canyons. The average daily sediment load was 500,000 tons, enough to fill a hundred freight trains, each with a hundred cars, with each car bearing a load of 200,000 pounds.

Some of this desert dirt settled out in the calm and smooth stretches of the river above the major cataracts, forming each year new beaches and sandbars, which were soon colonized by scores of ephemeral plants, milkweeds and datura, bear grass, and evening primroses. But much of the silt and sand flushed the length of the river, through Marble

Canyon and the Grand, only coming to a rest below the last of the great rapids, some two hundred miles from the Gulf of California, where the gradient finally leveled off and the river slowed. Here it built up, so dramatically that the riverbed itself would rise year by year, as if the entire vast delta lay poised on a hydraulic lift. Inevitably and unpredictably the Colorado, constrained only by banks of silt, would break through and, with the power of a flood, forge new paths to the sea. Over the millennia these routes were revisited time and again, with some channels flowing south into what became Mexico, and others favoring a northerly course, away from the sea. There were times when gravity trumped geography and the river turned away from the ocean to disgorge to the north into a vast low basin of the Imperial Valley, where it formed an evanescent lake, the Salton Sea, today California's largest landlocked body of water. Then, as if an animate being, its whims satisfied, the river would within a few decades reverse its course and once again make its way for the sea, returning life to the delta.

As a result of these meanderings, Colorado River sediments became deposited over a vast area and to depths that promised enormous wealth to anyone who could learn to farm in the desert air. Yuma, Arizona, a historic river crossing just east of the California state line, is a hundred miles from the sea, but thanks to the accumulation of silt, it sits atop eighty feet of sediments which, if augmented by nitrogen and water, are transformed into some of the most fertile and productive soil in the United States. Statistically it is the sunniest place on the planet, and consistently the hottest city in the country, with summer temperatures averaging 117°F. Yuma receives a mere four inches of precipitation a year, and yet it is the lettuce capital of the world, producing 95 percent of the winter crop for all of North America. The water, of course, comes from the river, which means that nearly all of us, wherever we live in the country, drink from the Colorado virtually every day of our lives.

IN THE EARLY MORNING LIGHT the landing at Lees Ferry is fired with activity, as both private and commercial river expeditions scramble to get their rafts rigged and their clients ready to launch at the precise time allocated by the permitting process. For all the easy camaraderie, there is a palpable energy, a nervous excitement of anticipation and foreboding, that comes with the realization, especially for the private parties, some of whom have waited years for the privilege, that the river passage of their dreams is about to begin. The guides, weathered and sun-beaten, go about their tasks with an easy insouciance, while the clients flutter about in sun hats and brightly colored long-sleeved shirts, trying to be useful, pausing from time to time to slather on another layer of sunscreen, all the while chatting nervously about nothing in particular, as their eyes, hidden behind shades, dart back and forth between the parking lot and the river. Rows of late-model pickups overflow into a second lot, and a third. Some parties will travel only as far as Phantom Ranch, but most will go the distance to Diamond Creek, a fortnight's journey of 226 miles. No one travels light, and the steady stream of gear and food boxes moving toward the shore suggests a commando operation, fully equipped and a bit excessive.

Our party is completely over the top. Forty-four men and women, half-a-dozen world-class kayakers, not one but two IMAX film crews (one just to handle the 3D camera), miscellaneous executives from Teva, models and set designers, and a brave photographer hired to shoot the corporate sponsor's ad campaign, several tons of equipment, along with guides and swampers for two dories, five oar rafts, three snout boats, and two enormous unspecified rigs that seem to stretch as long as the river is wide. We are the largest group in years to be approved by the National Park Service for a descent of the Canyon, and even before setting off we have been told that we will be the last. Apparently never again will such an enormous expedition slip through the permitting process.

As another private party of dories sets off, heading down toward the mouth of the Paria River and into Marble Canyon, large motorized snout boats land at the dock from upriver, disgorging thirty or forty passengers at a time, families for the most part, who have enjoyed a four-hour outing from a landing beneath the vaulted arch of the Glen Canyon Dam. Children scamper toward the rafts and stare in wonder at the guides while their parents walk slowly uphill over the asphalt toward the waiting buses. A long queue forms outside the public toilets.

Fly fishermen on the shore await launches that will carry

Glen Canyon, June 1915, prior to the erection of the Glen Canyon Dam, which began in 1956.

Left to Right: *Regan Dale, Robert F. Kennedy, Jr., Tara Davis, and Kick Kennedy on the river in a traditional dory*

them upstream, where in cool, clear waters in the shadow of dense thickets of tamarisk they will flog the back-eddies and pools of what has become one of the premier trophy-trout fisheries in the United States. Before the dams this stretch of the Colorado would never have harbored trout. The water temperatures then ranged from near freezing in winter to bathtub warm in the summer. The river, originally named for its color, deep red like the desert sand, was so weighted down with sediment that it was said to be "too thick to drink and too thin to plough." Now the silt settles above the Glen Canyon Dam in a reservoir called Lake Powell. The water released to become a river comes from two hundred feet below the surface and is a constant 47°F, an ideal temperature for trout. If a person resting on a raft in the afternoon sun slips into the river, they experience a sudden temperature drop of as much as seventy degrees, in conditions that can induce hypothermia within five minutes. This can be tough on clients, but it is far worse for the native fish, the chub and suckers, and the squawfish that once grew to six feet and weighed in at eighty pounds. Of the twenty-one species of fish found today in the Colorado only six are native. Fifteen are introduced. Of the eight species once native to the Canyon, five were endemic, and all of these are now moribund or extinct.

MOTORING UP THE COLORADO from Lees Ferry beneath the undulating bluffs of Navajo Sandstone, exquisite and massive beyond imaginings, with the morning light on the rock and a thin veil of mist hovering over the water, one feels a strange contradiction. You want to hate this place, said by all conventional wisdom to have been ruined by the erection of the dam. And, impressive as this remnant stretch of the Glen Canyon may be, one invariably thinks of what was lost beyond the dam: the cliffs and folding sandstone of the endless chasms and canyons, the alcoves, seeps, and grottos, the ruins and memories of the Anasazi, the Ancient Ones, all drowned beneath the waters of a reservoir. And yet there is an inherent beauty to the crystal green waters, a superficial appeal in the

stable stands of wispy tamarisk by the shores. It is a more welcoming river than the raging Colorado of old, with its psychotic fluctuations, its murky water impossible to bathe in, let alone drink.

But this is exactly the problem. One is drawn to the modern river largely because it is so welcoming, its water clear and clean, its flows scientifically controlled and predictable. River guides here do not watch the clouds and the weather to anticipate the dawn. They make satellite phone calls to technicians to learn of power demands and releases, timed to the minute, with charts that measure not the frontier reaches of dreams and the imagination but the precise and certain trajectories of the artificial tides that, once released, run down the chasm of the canyon with the predictability of a well-engineered machine.

I was reminded of this when we went to Lake Powell to spend several days on a luxury houseboat, filming from the surface of the reservoir. The two-storied vessels, which rent for $2,000 a day, come equipped with climate-controlled central air conditioning, DVDs and plasma televisions on every deck and in every room, several fully equipped bars, a well-appointed kitchen, and, on the top deck, a hot tub and a plastic slide. As you motor out from the marina, with its acres of ramps and moorings, increasingly distant from the shore as the reservoir drops with every month of drought, you join a steady stream of recreational machines, motor craft, and houseboats of all sizes, heading like a naval convoy out onto the blue surface of a body of water at one point 186 miles long, with a shoreline that would stretch from Seattle to San Diego. There are Jet Skis and racing boats everywhere, roaring from gasoline pump to gasoline pump, dragging behind them boys and girls on water skis, screaming with delight.

Fewer than twenty-five thousand people a year raft the Colorado River from Lees Ferry to Diamond Creek. Over 3.5 million come to Lake Powell. The guides on the reservoir, affable and content with their paunches, cigarettes, and coolers of beer, are of a different breed from those encountered on the river. They too are good and decent people, but their fraternity has been forged by a psychic disconnect. They seem not to notice that what they call an island is in fact a drowned butte. What they describe as a lake is a man-made reservoir, so transparently artificial that as the water recedes it leaves a

white stain on the red Navajo Sandstone, as conspicuous as the ring left in a bathtub as the wash water drains. They make no mention, and perhaps, given their age, do not even know, of the drowned beauty, the glens and hidden recesses that lie beneath their recreational playground. The death of Glen Canyon is widely perceived by the elders of the American environmental movement as one of the most egregious acts of betrayal in the history of the country, "the greatest fraud," as photographer Elliot Porter wrote, "ever perpetrated by responsible government on an unsuspecting people." This jewel of a canyon, a birthright for all, was destroyed before the American people even knew they possessed it. "No man-made artifact in all of human history," wrote Edward Abbey, "has been hated by so many for so long as the Glen Canyon Dam."

What is most disturbing today is the realization that the commercial operators on Lake Powell have no memory of what once was, nor any evident interest in that history. The fluidity of their memory, their capacity to forget, is complete. They and their clients seek, as Porter bitterly remarked, "artificial thrills to lessen the drag of time, side-slipping in tight S-turns at thirty miles an hour." But, as Porter lamented, the truth remains. In place of a living river is a dead reservoir, a featureless sheet of water, a moribund basin that accumulates all the flotsam from the surrounding land, a sink for sediments and trash, and a burial ground for the wild.

Balanced Rock, a well-know landmark on the road to Lees Ferry

IN 1539, TWO YEARS BEFORE HERNÁNDO CORTÉS SENT FRANCISCO DE ULLOA UP THE PACIFIC COAST TO LOOK FOR CALIFORNIA, A LEGENDARY KINGDOM OF BLACK WOMEN RULED BY A QUEEN NAMED CALIFIA, DON FRANCISCO VÁSQUEZ DE Coronado set out from Guadalajara, also heading north, with two hundred horsemen in search of Cíbola, one of the fabled Seven Cities, where houses and streets were said to be paved with gold. Like El Dorado and the Fountain of Youth, these were both imaginary destinations, derived for the most part from Greek myth, and imposed by the feverish minds of the Conquistadors on the virgin landscape of a New World.

Coronado's quixotic wanderings took him through lands once dominated by the Hohokam, a desert civilization that had collapsed around AD 1400, and across the uplands of the Mogollon Rim to the ruinous plains of West Texas, Oklahoma, and Kansas. There was no gold to be found, and no other wealth beyond the kernels of maize and the odd turquoise necklace and obsidian blade. The expedition in the end was important not for what it brought back but for what was left behind, the Arabian and Andalusian horses that allowed the peoples of the Great Plains—the Kiowa, Comanche, Arapaho, Cheyenne, Apache, Lakota, and the Crow—to forge a new way of life, a hunting culture based on the buffalo and inspired by the divinity of the sun.

In the midst of his journey, a passage of deprivation and annihilation for which Coronado would be fully prosecuted under Spanish law, his second in command, Captain López de Cárdenas, stumbled upon the Grand Canyon of the Colorado, reaching the South Rim somewhere between Desert View and Moran Point in late September of 1540. Unimpressed and irritated by such an impediment to his progress, he stared into the abyss and saw at the bottom a narrow ribbon of water that he estimated to be a mere eight feet wide. He dispatched three of his men to investigate. They reached but a third of the way down to the canyon floor before retreating in horror and fear, their sense of scale and perspective shattered by the

experience. Cárdenas later reported the canyon's existence to Coronado, dismissing it and the entire region as a "useless piece of country." The Spanish imagination was prepared to discover cities of gold, forest kingdoms of one-breasted women, and black queens. But the Grand Canyon of the Colorado was something else, a chasm that defied reason, an actual place so vast it could swallow Seville and obliterate every trace and memory.

More than two centuries would pass before another European face encountered the canyon's void. In July of 1776, the month America was born, two priests, Father Silvestre Vélezde Escalante and Francisco Domínguez, set out from Santa Fe in search of an overland route through the canyonlands to Monterey, California. They never found it. Lost, beaten by the sun and frozen by winter blizzards, they survived by eating their mules and sucking moisture from plants. The end of November found them wandering the north rim of the canyon, above Marble Canyon, seeking a crossing and a way home to the mission at Santa Fe. Cutting steps in the sandstone cliffs with an axe, they forged a route to the floor of Glen Canyon and discovered a ford, later known as the Crossing of the Fathers, which today, of course, lies inundated by the reservoir.

Later travelers, fur traders and trappers in the 1820s, military expeditions in the 1850s, found the region to be equally uninviting. In 1857 the War Department sent Lieutenant Joseph Christmas Ives in a stern-wheeler up the Colorado from the Gulf of California to determine the river's highest point of navigation. After two months and 350 miles he ran aground in Black Canyon, some twenty miles below the present site of Hoover Dam. Ives and his men abandoned the vessel and set off east into the Grand Canyon, exploring Diamond Creek and eventually making their way along the South Rim to a point above the confluence of the main river and its notable affluent, the Little Colorado. In 1861 Ives published his expedition account, *Report Upon the Colorado River of the West*. He had not been impressed. "The region," he wrote, "is, of course, altogether valueless. It can be approached only from the south, and after entering it there is nothing to do but leave. Ours has been the first, and will doubtless be the last, party of whites to visit this profitless locality. It seems intended

Yaki Point blanketed with snow

by nature that the Colorado River, along the greater portion of its lonely and majestic way, shall be forever unvisited and undisturbed."

The Colorado, of course, was not without worth, nor would it remain unvisited. Even as Ives ascended the river from below, there were others exploring its possibilities from above. In 1846 Brigham Young and his Mormon followers had settled the shores of the Great Salt Lake, ending an arduous pilgrimage that had taken the Latter Day Saints across the empty wilderness of an entire continent. Their spiritual quest, like that of the many millenarian religious movements that flashed in the frontier imagination of nineteenth-century America, had been born of the fantasies of a conflicted yet inspired visionary.

According to Mormon history, the founder of the faith, Joseph Smith, the son of an impoverished New England farmer, was visited in 1827 by an angel named Moroni, who presented him with golden plates inscribed with sacred messages. With the use of special stones set into silver, Smith was able to translate these metaphysical texts into the Book of Mormon. The scriptures unveiled the promise of a new religious order, a faith inspired by revelation, in which God had evolved from man, man could become God, the soul predated birth, and the dead could be saved and resurrected through the rite of baptism. Among the other startling discoveries was the revealed knowledge that Christ had visited the Americas after his crucifiction, and that the tribes of Israel had migrated to the United States long before his birth, and that their descendants were still alive, the myriad Indian peoples of the American West.

Such provocative beliefs proved unsettling to some, and wherever Smith and his acolytes moved, they generated and encountered hostility. Persecution only reinforced the Mormon sense of isolation and their notion of being a chosen people endowed with a unique mission, the building of a new world order, a new Zion. They tried Ohio and then Missouri before settling in Illinois, where Smith oversaw the construction of the new city of Nauvoo. When, in 1844, a deranged adversary murdered Smith, his deputy, Brigham Young, decided to abandon the settled reaches of the Midwest and embark with his fellow believers on a migration west, a hegira that would not end, he vowed, until he, as the sole

conduit to the angels, would receive a message from God. The destination was an imagined land of Zion, a sacred calling that in time led the Latter Day Saints not only to the shores of the Great Salt Lake but also, through a systematic plan of expansion and colonization, throughout the Great Basin and beyond.

Some colonists moved north toward Idaho and south along the Wasatch Range to the far reaches of the Colorado Plateau. Other thrusts went west along the Old Spanish Trail toward Southern California, and south through Arizona to the Mexican frontier. The strategic hope of the Mormon leadership was to forge a new empire in the heart of the continent, a Kingdom of Zion, fertile, transformed, and green, with its capital to be a New Jerusalem, a shining city from where the Mormon gospel, invented in a cornfield in New England, might spread to every nation and people on Earth.

At the forefront of the empire were the missionary scouts, devoted frontiersmen whose duty was to explore the unknown plateaus and canyons, find sources of water in the desert, and forge alliances with the Indian nations, such that their land

Marble Canyon, viewed from the hills below the Nankoweap Granary

might be settled and the people themselves brought into the fold of the faith. In 1854 Brigham Young dispatched Jacob Hamblin, a close confidant of the Mormon leader, to treat with the Paiute Indians and to find a ford of the Colorado River that might allow for the penetration of the lands of the Hopi and Navajo, and the other peoples of the southern canyons, the Havasupai and Hualapai. Hamblin found two crossings of the Colorado, one below Grand Wash Cliffs at the lower end of the Grand Canyon and another at the mouth of the Paria River, just above Marble Canyon and below the last walls of what would become known as Glen Canyon.

The Paiute were a Water People, originally from the Great Basin, who had migrated to the north rim of the Canyon around AD 1300. A hunting and gathering culture, they lived simply in brush shelters, dependent largely on wild plants, mesquite pods, cactus fruit, and the hearts of agaves, which they rendered edible by roasting them for days in rock-lined pits under a blanket of juniper branches. Though their material culture was rudimentary, Paiute beliefs were complex and their sense of place complete. They knew that springs and rocks, rivers and rain had life spirits that had to be honored. They viewed the entire Grand Canyon as something holy. Their name for their sacred homeland was Puaxantu Tuvip, a term that implied a landscape vibrant, alive, and responsive in a thousand ways to human needs and aspirations.

Such beliefs intrigued Jacob Hamblin, who as a missionary was sympathetic to any religious conviction, even those he intended to transform. The genesis of the Grand Canyon was to him quite obvious. The Book of Mormon made it clear that the Earth, and indeed existence itself, had begun some six thousand years ago, a depth of time that was beyond the imaginings of an acolyte of a religion not yet thirty years old. The Grand Canyon, the Mormon faith maintained, had come into being in a single moment when the world had been cleaved by the earthquakes that heralded the crucifixion of Christ.

Hamblin took a Paiute woman as one of his four wives, and went on to attempt to evangelize the Hopi and the Navajo. The Navajo had come to the canyonlands late, arriving around AD 1600, exhausted by an epic migration that had brought them, an Athapaskan people, south in five hundred years from the northern reaches of a continent to the desert sands of the Southwest. This did not stop them from metaphysically embracing the Grand Canyon. To the contrary, even as they opportunistically learned to work silver and herd sheep, they reinvented their mythology. They already knew that their people had originated in a series of underworlds, only to emerge on the surface of a planet covered with water. When this cosmic flood receded, it left in its wake the Grand Canyon. Thus with every ritual cycle the Navajo make prayers to the Canyon and the River, which is seen as an animate being, a male essence that forever flows toward its female consort, the Little Colorado, the tributary whose waters mingle so effortlessly in the current of the greater stream.

To the Mormons such notions were nonsensical. Their mission, inspired by God, was to settle and make fertile the desert wastes. Anyone who challenged this destiny was suspect. In early September of 1857 Jacob Hamblin and the Apostle George A. Smith were returning from a southern sojourn, having been dispatched by Brigham Young to warn the Mormon cadre not to engage in commerce with the wagon trains and the settlers passing through their territory en route to the Pacific. At Corn Creek near the Utah town of Filmore, Hamblin encountered a party of families from Arkansas led by a man named Fancher, heading west with their wagons for California. Hamblin suggested they make camp further to the south, in the gentle grassy terrain of a place he called Mountain Meadows, not far from his own home. Then, by his account, he moved on, returning to his family in Salt Lake. Within days some 120 people—every man, woman, and child old enough to be capable of remembering—lay dead in the meadow, killed not by Indians but by Mormons. Only children too young to talk were spared, and these were herded for adoption into the family of the Latter Day Saints.

The perpetrators of the slaughter scattered, and the Mormon Church did little to bring them to justice. Only when word of the massacre reached Washington and the United States government, after years of passivity, exerted its sovereignty, threatening the very existence of the Mormon state, did Brigham Young bring frontier justice to bear. Of the many perpetrators, he chose to isolate one as the scapegoat, his own adopted son, John Doyle Lee, a prosperous trader and husband of nineteen women, whom he formally banished in 1872. Excommunicated from the Church, Lee came south with just

two of his wives to settle at the remote Colorado River crossing discovered by Jacob Hamblin just above the Paria confluence, the landing that today bears Lee's name. It was a bleak, sun-beaten flat, a devil's anvil, with no shelter from the sun. An eastern politician who later visited the site noted that he too, if dispatched to such a dreary spot, would be inclined to embrace polygamy.

Lee and his women arrived at the crossing in 1871 and, secretly financed by the Mormon Church, immediately set to work, establishing a ferry, erecting a trading post to attract the Navajo, digging irrigation ditches, and planting fruit trees to provide a touch of shade. One of the women, his seventeenth bride, named their ranch Lonely Dell. For a time they prospered, controlling as they did the only ferry crossing on the Colorado between Utah and California. But eventually U.S. law caught up with them and John Lee was sacrificed upon the altar of Utah statehood, becoming the only Mountain Meadows murderer to be executed for his crimes. He died by firing squad on March 23, 1877. Two years later his wife Emma Lee sold the ferry for a hundred milk cows to the Mormon Church, which continued to run it until 1910, when the operation was taken over by the Coconino County government. The ferry closed in 1928, when the Navajo Bridge was built a few miles downriver across Marble Canyon. For more than fifty years Lees Ferry had provided the only access to all of the lands south of the Colorado, the conduit through which passed every Mormon missionary intent upon the transformation of the ancient peoples of the desert, the Hopi, Navajo, the Havasupai and Hualapai and, of course, the Zuni.

A sunrise at Mather Point

Zoroaster Temple

Marble Canyon, seen from above, with Shinumo Altar in the distance, by J. K. Hillers

THE ZUNI FIRST SAW THE WORLD WHEN THEIR ANCESTORS, TOGETHER WITH THOSE OF THE HAVASUPAI AND HUALAPAI, EMERGED FROM THE WOMB OF THE EARTH NEAR A PLACE NOW KNOWN AS Ribbon Falls in the heart of the Grand Canyon. To this day their prayers recall their astonishment as they took in the canyon's beauty, the painted rocks and magical animals, the springs and lush plantings by the shallows of Bright Angel Creek, the fulcrum of creation on the canyon's rim where they first saw sunlight crack open the sky. Inspired by what they encountered in this, the fourth realm, the world of light, they began to wander in search of the ideal home, Idiwana'a, the Middle Place, where perfect balance and stability might be found. They journeyed first to the east, stopping at four sacred springs, and then moved up the Little Colorado, planting corn, building villages, and erecting shrines, where they made offerings and buried their elders who had passed away. At the confluence of the Little Colorado and the Zuni, they encountered the Kokko, a host of supernatural beings. The place became sacred, encoded for all time in Zuni memory as the destination of the dead. Moving on, they reached the headwaters of the river that today bears their name, and there they at last found Idiwana'a, where they settled for all time.

Countless generations later, the Zuni are still there. Their religious celebrations continue as they always have, with each ritual gesture being a prayer for the stability and prosperity of the Earth and all its inhabitants. Their origin myths and all of their stories tell nothing of angels and golden tablets, or of new lands to conquer and deserts to transform. Their memories register nothing of lost tribes and chosen peoples. There is no mention of a Zion in the canon of Zuni lore.

This is not to say that their mythological beliefs are any less fantastical than those of the Mormons. But it does suggest that there are different ways of interpreting reality, and that how a people conceive of themselves and their place on the Earth reveals much about their values and priorities, the metaphors and intuitions that propel them forward. The Zuni accepted existence, as it was, a perfect expression of the primordial beings, Sun Father and Moonlight-Giving Mother, the ultimate custodians of light and life. They live with that knowledge and, as a consequence, have no interest in changing or improving upon the world that embraced their ancestors and sheltered and nurtured them as infants. They look and see and accept.

The Mormons, by contrast, celebrated an ideology of transformation. The entire purpose of human life is to change the nature of the planet, rendering the wild tame, making safe and bountiful the lives of the living. Cast adrift from the lands of their origins, tormented and persecuted for a failure to conform to an orthodox world their revelations defied, they survived by becoming the absolute masters of their destiny. It was no accident that Brigham Young, inspired by the angels, elected to settle in the most barren landscape imaginable. He had asked of his flock the impossible. Through every kind of adversity and danger, they had walked the breadth of a continent, enduring tornado winds, the wrath of wild and savage tribes, the physical challenges of rivers in flood, and tall-grass prairies where dense thickets rose higher than their wagons. Only a land as barren as the salt flats of Utah could provide a rough coefficient of what they had already endured and achieved, and thus redeem and affirm the fundamental truth of their spiritual convictions.

Once committed to place, they worked furiously to transform it. Within days they attacked the desert, and within two generations had brought six million acres under cultivation, all by harnessing and transporting water. Their success inspired many, including politicians and speculators in the East, who maintained the Jeffersonian ideal of America as a rural farming nation, in which every man might be granted his own domain, 160 acres upon which to build a life.

It was a proud notion, a venerable part of the American myth, and one that had worked well east of the 100th Meridian. But beyond that longitude, it was sheer fantasy. As John Wesley

No matter how far you have wandered hitherto, or
how many famous gorges and valleys you have seen,
this one, the Grand Cañon of the Colorado, will
seem as novel to you, as unearthly in the color and
grandeur and quantity of its architecture, as if you
have found it after death, on some other star.

—John Muir, *Our National Parks*, 1901

Water pools in the Esplanade on the North Rim

Powell would so eloquently suggest, the issue in the West was not soil or land, but water. With water, 160 acres might be too much for a man to manage. But without it even ten thousand acres, a fiefdom of a lord, could leave a family destitute. Powell's views were heretical to those calling for the settlement of the West, such as Horace Greeley, the New York newspaperman who popularized the iconic slogan "Go West Young Man, Go West." Greeley preferred the rhetoric of men such as William Gilpin, a bombastic orator who claimed, in absolute defiance of reality, that, "in readiness to receive and ability to sustain in perpetuity a dense population the West is more favored than Europe."

Promotional schemes of both government and the railroads went as far as to perpetrate the curious idea, which they cloaked in the language of nineteenth-century science, that rainfall followed the plough and that the very act of tilling the western soils would in and of itself cause rain to fall. This transparently idiotic notion was embraced through the late 1880s with the certainty of dogma. By the time such foolishness was exposed by harsh reality, it was in a sense too late. The country, in defiance of all logic, had become blindly committed to the agrarian settlement of the desert West. If the land itself refused to generate rain, the only option was to bring the rain to the land, and that meant irrigation and on a scale previously unimagined.

In 1902, six years after Utah attained statehood, the United States government launched the Bureau of Reclamation, an agency that in time would become virtually the sole public arbiter of water policy in the states west of the 100th Meridian. Inspired by the early Mormon successes, guided by Mormon laws and principles, and run in its early years largely by Mormons, the Bureau set out essentially to create Zion, using all the tools of the modern state. There was, of course, interest in flood control and power generation, but the primary goal was the greening of the desert, a purpose that over time took on Biblical resonance.

In 1953, President Dwight Eisenhower selected Ezra Taft Benson to become the Secretary of Agriculture. It was a controversial appointment. Benson's politics were rabidly conservative, far to the right of Eisenhower's. Benson came from Utah, a state whose contribution to the farm economy at the time was trivial. He was also the first clergyman to be asked to serve in a presidential cabinet in more than a hundred years. Among his many

Russell Sturges of the Teva kayaking team leaps into the river below while Regan Dale, Wade Davis, and Tara Davis look on

published books were such titles as *Come Unto Christ*; *Missionaries to Match Our Message*; *The Constitution: A Heavenly Banner*; *God, Family, Country: Our Three Great Loyalties*; and *A Witness and a Warning: A Modern-Day Prophet Testifies of the Book of Mormon*. Before accepting the offer from the president of the United States, Benson had to obtain permission from the president of the Mormon Church, one David O. McKay. At the time of Eisenhower's offer, Benson already had a full-time job, an appointment for life as a member of the secret Quorum of the Twelve Apostles, the supreme governing body of the Church of the Latter Day Saints.

Ezra Benson served Eisenhower for eight years, and played a powerful role in all policy concerning agriculture and the transformation of the desert West. He believed that the United States was a nation uniquely favored by God, and that the Constitution had been divinely inspired. His zeal reflexively acknowledged that man was destined to dominate nature, possessed of a heavenly mandate to rework the Earth for the benefit of all human beings, his countrymen in particular. In choosing Benson to be the face of American agriculture, Eisenhower, a son of Kansas, was sending a powerful signal that the future of farming lay in the transformation of the desert West. The key, as always in lands beyond the 100th Meridian, was water. In his opening sentence to his foreword for the 1955 *Yearbook of Agriculture*, Benson wrote, "I have little need to remind you that water has become one of our major national concerns." With powerful figures such as Ezra Taft Benson providing inspiration and political cover, the efforts of the Bureau of Reclamation to tame the Colorado became less a technical challenge than a national mission.

In 1922 representatives of the seven states that shared the Colorado River had reached an agreement that defined and apportioned water rights and obligations. The Colorado River Compact divided the river drainage into two zones, the Upper Basin, comprising Colorado, New Mexico, Utah, and Wyoming, and the Lower Basin, which included Nevada, California, and Arizona. The goal was to divide the total water volume of the river, estimated at the time to be roughly 16.4 million acre-feet per year, equitably between the two halves of the basin. The agreement, authorized by the U.S. Congress in the same year, granted 7.5 million acre-feet to each of the two designated regions, leaving a reserve of 1.4 million to satisfy the Mexicans,

who also had a claim to the river. Missing from the analysis was the fact that, in time, the combined surfaces of the reservoirs on the Colorado would lose to evaporation 2 million acre-feet of water every year. What's more, the figure of 16.4 million acre-feet per year was an estimate based on the observation and measurement of flows in a decade now generally recognized as having been one of abnormally high rainfall. The long-term flow of the Colorado is more likely to be on the order of 13.5 million acre-feet per year, a shortfall of nearly 3 million. The recent drought, which has resulted in reservoirs dropping to historic lows, may not be a drought at all, but merely a return to a drier climatic regime more typical of the historical pattern for the region.

None of this could have been foreseen in 1922 and, even as evidence of the miscalculation came to light in subsequent decades, no one, certainly no state authority, rushed to return water to the commons. To the contrary, once these allotments were granted they became carved in stone, and the entire thrust of state and federal government policies was to ensure that the obligations would be met. Further agreements, such as the Upper Colorado River Basin Compact of 1948, empowered the Bureau of Reclamation to do whatever it deemed necessary to guarantee the delivery of water. It was, in effect, a mandate to reconfigure and envision anew the entire basin of the Colorado.

Eight years later the U.S. Congress passed the Upper Colorado River Storage Project Act, which codified and endorsed the engineering plans proposed by the Bureau of Reclamation. The language of the bill was dense and complex, but it essentially sanctioned the construction of as many dams as were required to store in the upper reaches of the river as much water as was necessary to satisfy in perpetuity the demands and entitlements of everyone, but primarily those living in the economically thriving states of the lower river, most especially California.

That such an audacious plan could even be contemplated reveals how far the engineering of massive dams had advanced in two generations. In 1900 there was not a single dam in the world higher than fifteen meters. By 1950 there were 5,270. Thirty years later there would be 36,562. Today, worldwide, there are more than 800,000 dams, 40,000 of which are at least fifteen meters in height. Over the last fifty years, on average, every twelve hours has seen the completion of a dam on a scale unimaginable at the turn of the twentieth century.

The first, and the inspiration for all, was Boulder, later known as the Hoover Dam, which was initially envisioned in 1922 during the deliberations leading up to the signing of the Colorado River Compact. The plan was to plug the Black Canyon of the Colorado with a concrete gravity-arch structure of a size and height unlike anything that had ever been constructed. Authorized by Congress in 1928, the first contracts were awarded in the spring of 1931 to six companies, including Morrison-Knudsen of Boise, Idaho; the Utah Construction Company of Ogden, Utah; the Pacific Bridge Company of Portland, Oregon; and the Henry J. Kaiser and W. A. Bechtel companies of Oakland, California. None of these had ever attempted anything remotely like the task at hand. That the dam was completed in five years was a miracle of logistics and engineering, a pure act of national will.

Virtually every construction technique had to be invented on the spot by ordinary men, road builders for the most part, who knew little about dams, and what little they knew at the outset was largely irrelevant on a project of such a scale. The temporary cofferdam, built to divert the river from the construction site, would alone have been among the largest dams ever built had it been left standing. Excavations for the foundation of

the actual dam required the removal of 1.5 million cubic yards of material. To divert the river's flow around the construction site, four tunnels, each nearly sixty feet in diameter, had to be driven a total of sixteen thousand feet through the canyon walls. The dam itself, the largest structure ever built, required sixty-six million tons of concrete, which left alone to cure would have taken 125 years to set because of the heat generated by the sheer weight and mass of cement. Thus it became necessary to lace the concrete with cooling coils, enough to build a refrigeration plant that would stretch from the dam site, thirty miles southeast of Las Vegas, to San Diego. When the dam was finished, the entire flow of the Colorado ran through its turbines, the water reaching speeds of some eighty-five miles per hour as it dropped through the penstocks.

An engineering marvel, the Hoover Dam was stunningly beautiful, as transcendent in form and architecture as a great cathedral, with elegant Art Deco appointments and sculptured turrets rising seamlessly from it face. The monument built to celebrate the completion of the dam featured two thirty-foot winged figures of bronze, images of eagles ascending like Icarus, flanking a flagpole rising over 140 feet from its base of black diorite stone. Surrounding the base is a terrazzo floor, inlaid with a star chart, a celestial map that recalls the alignment of the heavens on the day, September 30, 1935, when Franklin D. Roosevelt dedicated the dam. Built at the height of the Great Depression at tremendous cost of treasure and blood, the Hoover Dam was more than a technical achievement. It was a symbol of national redemption and hope, a sign that in America, whatever the immediate challenges, anything could be accomplished.

Inspired as art and architecture, and producing enough electricity to bring into being entire cities in the desert, the Hoover Dam was nevertheless almost immediately beset with problems, which in turn set in motion a chain reaction of further construction. Lake Mead, the reservoir created by the dam and named for Elwood Mead, who had supervised its construction, spread upriver for over a hundred miles, reaching nearly forty miles into the Grand Canyon, a broad and flat basin of water that captured every pound of Colorado River silt. Within thirty-five years Lake Mead had more acre-feet of sediment than 98 percent of the reservoirs in the United States had acre-feet of water.

Right: *Glen Canyon Dam*
Below: *The Bureau of Reclamation opens the Glen Canyon Dam bypass tubes on November 21, 2004*

The solution was to build more dams, upstream. The Bureau had recommended as part of the Upper Colorado Basin Project a dam at Echo Park that would have inundated part of Dinosaur National Monument, close to the Colorado and Utah state line. The very thought of violating such a designated treasure galvanized the Sierra Club, whose members had never forgotten the damming of the Hetch Hetchy valley in Yosemite, the ecological outrage that had birthed the modern environmental movement. In a deal that he would regret for the rest of his life, David Brower, then head of the Sierra Club, agreed in 1956 not to oppose plans to dam Glen Canyon, provided the Bureau of Reclamation kill the project at Echo Park. The Bureau was secretly delighted, for Glen Canyon was the priority, a site that would allow for a massive reservoir capable of storing some twenty-four million acre-feet, fully 80 percent of all the water of the Upper Basin. What's more, a dam at Glen Canyon would both mitigate the sediment problem in Lake Mead by capturing the silt far upstream and also open up the possibility of a series of other projects reaching all through the Grand Canyon, with major dams proposed for Marble and Bridge Canyons. Had this scheme been realized, fully two-thirds of the Colorado's flow through the Grand Canyon would have stopped. The river would have become a series of reservoirs.

Work on the Glen Canyon Dam began in 1959 and by September 1963 ten million tons of concrete, poured over nearly four years, had been crafted into a 710-foot-high arch and gravity dam, which curved back into the river for strength, reaching 1,560 feet across the canyon as it rose from a base 350 feet thick. The gates closed in 1963, and the waters of Lake Powell began slowly to rise, inundating the timeless beauty of Glen Canyon, the rapids of Cataract Canyon, and thousands of ancient Anasazi ruins. When the dam was formally dedicated in 1966, fourteen years before the reservoir reached its full capacity, there were no celebrations of national pride and redemption. Already the consequences of the decision to build the dam were being felt. Senator Barry Goldwater, who had secured the funds to complete the project, would later regret his decision and call the construction of the dam a mistake. Edward Abbey wrote that the flooding of Glen Canyon was the equivalent of burying the Taj Mahal or Chartres Cathedral in mud until only the spires remained visible. Abbey was not alone in later calling for the dam to be demolished.

As the public came to understand what had been sacrificed, momentum grew to protect what remained of the Grand Canyon. An advertisement placed by the Sierra Club in the *New York Times* and the *Washington Post* famously asked, "Should we also flood the Sistine Chapel so tourists can get nearer the ceiling?" A sense of outrage swept through the nation, and led ultimately to the cancellation of any plans to violate the river with dams at Marble Canyon or anywhere else within the National Park. As a chastened David Brower said, "If we can't save the Grand Canyon, what the hell can we save?"

Today the Glen Canyon Dam remains an object of disdain. Water flows freely down the dam's corners. Hundreds of seventy-five-foot bolts have been driven into the exfoliating sandstone to pin the wall together. In 1982 it nearly collapsed. Extreme weather conditions together with a high runoff from a heavy winter snowpack brought the height of the reservoir to 3,708 feet above sea level, less than an inch below the point where engineers believed all control might have been lost. Two thousand tons of water a second roared through the spillways on either side of the dam. Ominous rumbling sounds were heard and enormous blocks of rock and concrete crashed out of the spillways. The Bureau of Reclamation issued formal statements to assure the public, but privately engineers acknowledged that they had feared for the structure's integrity. Had it collapsed the consequences would have been catastrophic. But for some, such a disaster could not have come too soon.

THE RESERVOIR BEHIND Glen Canyon Dam is named for the bravest of all the river boatmen, John Wesley Powell, who, in 1869, led the first expedition down the Colorado River. He was a complex man who saw the promise of the West for settlement, even as he understood its limitations, given the scarcity of water and the dearth of rain. He admired what the Mormons had achieved in a generation through irrigation, but as a scientist he knew that all the water from all the rivers west of the 100th Meridian would never be enough to allow the Great American Desert to bloom. He dismissed as preposterous fanciful assertions about the inherent fertility of western lands, even as he called for the rational exploitation of what water resources were to be found. As a result, a century after his great achievement on the Colorado, his legacy would be invoked both by conservationists who sought restraint and engineers who championed the complete transformation of the river that he, more than anyone, had elevated in the American mind. What he would have thought of the reservoir named in his honor sixty years after his death by his twentieth-century acolytes at the Bureau of Reclamation remains unclear and certainly questionable.

What is certain is that John Wesley Powell found his muse in the wild Colorado. He wrote poetically of clouds playing above the water, rolling "down in great masses, filling the gorge with gloom," or hanging "aloft from wall to wall, covering the chasm with a roof of impending storm." Another passage describes a gust of wind sweeping up a draw, making a rift in the clouds to reveal all of the blue heavens, as streams of sunlight pour through, illuminating crags and pinnacles, towers and walls. "The clouds," he wrote, "are children of the heavens, and when they play among the rocks they lift them to the region above." The Grand Canyon was a wilderness of stone, he claimed, from which the gods could have quarried every mountain scattered upon the Earth.

Like Walt Whitman, who came a generation before him, and his contemporary John Muir, Powell was the product both of his circumstances and his own imagination, for just as the American frontier stretched the scale of the landscape, so it invited the reinvention of self. Raised the son of a poor itinerant preacher, Powell grew up literally on the open road, a wanderer. At nineteen he walked across Wisconsin, a journey of four months. A year later he rowed the length of the Mississippi, and then the Ohio and Illinois. Picking up knowledge from books and scholars encountered on the way, dropping in periodically to Wheaton and Oberlin colleges for short sojourns, never graduating, he taught himself geology and ethnography, acquiring from direct experience the honed eye of the naturalist. Unlike more sedentary students who take what they learn in the classroom and apply it to the world, Powell absorbed unfettered what he witnessed in nature, and only later examined it through the filter of established knowledge. Thus as a scientist he saw the world as it was, not how it was expected to be, and this more than any other trait of his intellect allowed him to make unique and novel contribu-

John Wesley Powell at his desk, 1896

tions to anthropology and, in particular, geology. In time he would serve as the founding director of both the United States Geological Survey and the Bureau of American Ethnology, a singular academic achievement.

But first came the crucible of the Civil War. Powell fought for the Union, rising from private to the rank of major. At Shiloh in 1862 a minie ball shattered his right arm, which was sawn off three days after the battle, leaving him with a stump of raw nerve endings, a chronic source of acute pain for the rest of his life. Despite the agony, he served throughout the war, fighting at Big Black River at Vicksburg and all the subsequent engagements of the Mississippi campaign. When finally the war ended, in bloody exhaustion at Appomattox Court-house, he, like so many veterans, was not about to settle down.

Accompanied by his war-crazed brother Walter, a psychic casualty of a Confederate prison camp, Powell headed for Wyoming in 1867 with the goal of exploring for the first time the one remaining blank spot on the map of the American West. The canyonlands of Utah and Arizona had been penetrated, and men had traveled up the Colorado River as far as Diamond Creek, and down from the headwaters as far as the confluence of the Green and the Grand, where at the time the Colorado proper was said to begin. But no one had attempted to go further down into the void where the river, hidden in canyons, flowed for more than four hundred miles, dropping in that distance some 2,500 feet in elevation, a rate of descent twenty-five times that of the Mississippi. What Powell proposed was a journey into the unknown. Uncertainty would haunt every moment, with each bend in the river holding the promise of either deliverance or disaster.

In preparation for the expedition, Powell spent the winter of 1868–69 exploring the Green River country, living among the Ute Indians, studying their language, all the while waiting for the spring and the arrival of his boats, which had been ordered from the East and were scheduled to be delivered on the new transcontinental railroad. The Indians clearly admired Powell, who they named Kapurats, "the armless one." They shared with him rumors of the canyons and the river, legends of whirlpools and rapids that could swallow small mountains, caverns where the water disappeared beneath the Earth to flow unimpeded through the nether reaches of the underworld. The speed and direction of the river, the character of the rapids, the possible existence of high waterfalls or cataracts capable of tearing to splinters the timber of the craft, were, in fact, as unknown to the Indians as they were to him.

On May 24, 1869, Powell, with his party of ten men, embarked at Green River Station in the Wyoming Territory. They had three twenty-one-foot oak boats and one sixteen-foot pine skiff, with enough supplies to last them ten months. Before even reaching the confluence of the Grand, they lost one boat and most of their food. Within days one of the crew abandoned the expedition. Three more men would bolt from the depths of the canyon, at Separation Rapids, only to be killed three days later close to the rim, possibly by Shivwits Paiute Indians. Another boat, the one named for Powell's wife, the *Emma Dean*, had to be left behind on the shore. On August 30, thirteen weeks after setting out, with their supplies reduced to nothing but coffee and a few pounds of moldy flour and dried fruit, the expedition emerged from the Canyon near Grand Wash. Powell and his brother Walter made their way to a Mormon settlement at the mouth of the Virgin River and left the Colorado behind. Two of his men, Andy Hall and Billy Hawkins, re-supplied with food and ammunition, continued down the river to the Gulf of California, becoming the first to travel the Colorado all the way to the sea.

Powell emerged from the canyon a hero, and within days images of him strapped into his captain's chair, his fate tied literally to that of his vessel, the *Emma Dean*, appeared in the very newspapers that only weeks before had printed premature notices of his disappearance and death. Powell amused himself on his train journey east reading his obituaries. Once back in Washington he parlayed his new fame into a Congressional appropriation for a second expedition down the river. On May 22, 1871, with a decidedly more scientific team, Powell set off down the Green River, reaching Lees Ferry on October 23. They wintered over and resumed the journey on August 17, 1872, with the boatman Jack Hillers on this second leg of the exploration elevated to the position of expedition photographer. Going down the Canyon as far as Kanab Creek, they abandoned their boats on September 8 and walked out to the rim.

It would be more than two years before Powell would report his adventures in *Scribner's Weekly*, and in that time the Grand Canyon matured in his memory, taking on a mythic quality in his imagination that completely fused his destiny

with its glory. His *Report on the Exploration of the Colorado River of the West and Its Tributaries*, published by the Smithsonian in 1875, was written as a tale of adventure in the first person as if a daily journal of discovery, with events from all his expeditions employed indiscriminately to build a single dramatic narrative. Powell's actual journal notes were cryptic and truncated in the extreme, as one would expect from an expedition in constant peril and chaos. In his published report deep descriptions and lyrical flourishes abound, along with engravings that inflate every feature of a landscape that by its nature already defies hyperbole. His book was conceived quite deliberately to fire the hearts of Americans—and it did, elevating Powell and the Grand Canyon, both relative unknowns at the time, to the status of American icons.

Powell's boat, the Emma Dean, *with Hillers's chair for photographing, circa 1871*

THE GRANDEUR OF THE CANYON CONFERS DIGNITY ON EVERY FORM OF LIFE WITHIN ITS WALLS, EVEN DOWN UNTO THE MEANEST AND THE MOST PETTY. IT IS AN HONOR TO BE A VISITOR IN THE GRAND CANYON OF THE COLORADO, AS IT IS AN HONOR AND A PRIVILEGE TO BE ALIVE, HOWEVER BRIEFLY, ON THIS MARVELOUS PLANET WE CALL EARTH.

—EDWARD ABBEY, *ONE LIFE AT A TIME, PLEASE*, 1988

PHOTOGRAPHS OF POWELL TAKEN IN HIS PRIME, WITH TAU-GU, HIS PAIUTE GUIDE, IN THE DESERTS OF UTAH IN 1872, OR SEATED FOR A FORMAL PORTRAIT AS DIRECTOR OF THE GEOLOGICAL SURVEY A DECADE later in Washington, his long beard streaked in gray and covering his chest, suggest a leader of Biblical proportions. In fact, he was a small man, 5 feet 6½ inches tall, perhaps 120 pounds fully clothed, a "stick of beef jerky adorned with whiskers," as one biographer described him. But he had immense reservoirs of ambition, confidence, and strength, and, as his shining eyes in the portraits fully attest, he suffered from a uniquely American affliction, a pathological sense of optimism that broached no possibility of failure whatever the endeavor.

Powell appreciated from the start that the story of the Canyon was its geology, all of which was essentially new to science and of a scale that could well have intimidated a lesser man. But the same wild audacity that carried him downriver in the face of unimaginable perils endowed him with a quality and spirit of mind that allowed him to make sense of what he was seeing, which was no mean achievement. Even today travelers on the river, equipped with maps and books and prompted by river guides who know the entire story by rote, still struggle to identify its features and understand its geology. Imagine how it was in Powell's day: There were no reference points; nothing on Earth that could compare in scale, magnitude, and chronological depth to the world unveiled by the stratigraphy of the Canyon, bands of rock that soared in places a mile above the river. At the time most of the civilized world still maintained, as did the Mormons, that the Earth was six thousand years old. Scientists such as Powell were in the process of shattering that orthodoxy. In mere decades, the known age of the Earth would increase a millionfold, to 4.6 billion years.

The intensity of the intellectual shock wave unleashed by these scientific discoveries can only be imagined. To accept the revelations of geology effectively obliged one to accept the revelations of biology, for if rocks could change profoundly through time, so too could species. Geology provided the time frame that the mechanics of evolutionary theory demanded. Charles Darwin published *The Origin of Species* in 1859, a decade before Powell's Colorado expedition. This most profound and sweeping scientific theory was very much on his mind as he moved through the depths of the Canyon. To him the entire Grand Canyon was a "library of the gods," with each of its myriad draws and side canyons being separate reading rooms, dedicated to yet another natural wonder. "The shelves," he wrote, "are not for books, but form the stony leaves of one great book. He who would read the language of the universe may dig out letters here and there, and with them spell the words, and read, in a slow and imperfect way, but still so as to understand a little, the story of creation."

Powell did not reveal all of the mysteries of the Canyon. Indeed to this day important questions remain to be answered. But given the harrowing circumstances of his passage down the river, what he discovered is astonishing. He recognized, for example, that the river did not simply erode a path through the chasm of the Canyon, but that the land itself, a vast dome of rock of the Colorado Plateau, had been soaring upwards even as the river had been cutting down. Powell compared it to a saw spinning in place, as the log it was cutting kept rising slowly into the blade. He recognized the myriad erosive forces acting on the Canyon at all times. "Beds hundreds of feet in thickness and hundreds of thousands of square miles in extent," he wrote, "beds of granite and beds of schist, beds of marble and beds of sandstone, crumbling shale and adamantine lavas have slowly yielded to the silent and unseen powers of the air, and crumbled into dust and been washed away by the rains and carried into the sea by the rivers."

Perhaps most profoundly, Powell, as the writer John McPhee remarked, taught himself to think and to see in geologic time. Long before the scientific discovery of plate tectonics, before even the final acceptance of Darwinian theory, Powell envisioned the slow crawl of continents in motion, of

Powell with Tau-Gu, his guide and a member of the Paiute tribe, circa 1872

rivers being born of rain and running into lakes that through this scale of time were as evanescent as a drop of water on a sun-baked stone. Mountains as impermanent as sand castles, oceans sweeping over the land, leaving in their wake depositions of calcium carbonate, limestone a mile thick, all composed of the remnants of organisms the size of microns. He could look up at a rock face and see a hundred million years in a glance, or take a single step down across the strata, knowing full well that his feet had traversed sixty thousand years. Time, he understood, once embraced on a scale previously unimagined, could make anything possible.

We have cut through the sandstones and limestones met in the upper part of the canyon and through one great bed of marble a thousand feet in thickness. As this great bed forms a distinctive feature of the canyon, we call it Marble Canyon.

—John Wesley Powell, August 9, 1869

The wind-swept walls of Marble Canyon

✸ Night and day the river flows. If time is the mind of space, the Colorado is the soul of the desert. Brave boatmen come, they go, they die, and the voyage flows on forever. We are all canyoneers. We are all passengers on this little living mossy ship, this delicate dory sailing round the sun that humans call the Earth. ✸

—Edward Abbey, *The Hidden Canyon: A River Journey*, 1999

The Colorado River, seen from the foot of the Toroweap, by J. K. Hillers

In the Grand Canyon, there are thousands of gorges like that below Niagara Falls, and there are a thousand Yosemites. Pluck up Mt. Washington by the roots to the level of the sea and drop it headfirst into the Grand Canyon, and the dam will not force its waters over the walls. Pluck up the Blue Ridge and hurl it into the Grand Canyon, and it will not fill it.

—John Wesley Powell, *Canyons of the Colorado*, 1895

THE CANYON ENDURES THE TRIFLING BUSYNESS OF
HUMANS AS IT DOES THE INDUSTRY OF ANTS, THE
TRICKLE-DOWN EROSION OF SNOW AND FREEZE, THE
CASCADE OF FLOODS, THE TRANSIENT INSULT OF
GLEN CANYON DAM. THESE THINGS SHALL PASS. THE
CANYON WILL OUTLIVE THEM ALL.

—EDWARD ABBEY,
FOREWORD TO *A RIVER RUNNER'S GUIDE TO THE HISTORY
OF THE GRAND CANYON* BY KIM CRUMBO, 1981.

Mist and snow on the Bright Angel Trail

THE EARTH, WE NOW KNOW, WAS BORN OF STARDUST SOME 4.6 BILLION YEARS AGO, AS CLOUDS OF INTERSTELLAR GAS CAST INTO THE UNIVERSE BY THE SUPERNOVA EXPLOSION OF A GIANT STAR SPUN INTO being the sun and all the spheres of the solar system. In the beginning there was only heat and atomic matter, the molecular foundations of existence. But within 200 million years rocks had formed, and oceans, with a primordial crust covering the planet. Tectonic plates formed and the fundamental forces of movement, collision, subduction, and volcanic eruption, gradually created the mountainous profile of the world.

Some 2 billion years ago a small continent that would become the nucleus of North America moved to the south and east, pushing before it an oceanic crust that slipped beneath an adjacent plate, releasing vast streams of molten magma, which rose to form an arc of volcanic islands strung like fiery jewels across thousands of miles of ocean. Over the subsequent 200 million years the continent moved closer, even as the islands

The Grand Canyon, seen from space

came and went, a process of erosion and eruption that resulted in the accumulation of forty thousand feet of ash, sand, mud, and lava. When finally the continental plate drove beneath the island chain, the intense heat and pressure fused these deposits into metamorphic stone, rocks that became known to geologists as the Vishnu Schist. The magma infused in the volcanic columns and chambers solidified into Zoroaster Granite. These today form the primordial walls of the Inner Gorge of the Grand Canyon. To touch this stone is to reach back 1.8 billion years, well over a third of the history of the Earth.

The tremendous mountains uplifted and forged by this collision began to erode, and by 1.2 billion years ago the Vishnu Schist and Zoroaster Granite lay fully exposed, causing them, in turn, to slowly and imperceptibly slip away, resulting, after millions of years, in the creation of a flat sea-level plain. An ocean then spread upon the land. Life, which had originated over 2 billion years earlier, still consisted of single-celled bacteria that formed slimy mats on the sea floor. Organic and inorganic sediments from this primordial ocean created the Bass Limestone, and, as the sea slipped away, the mud deposited on its retreating shores left in its wake the Hakatai Shale. These, along with the pink cliffs of Shinumo Quartzite, forged from metamorphosed river and delta sands, and the Dox Formation of sand and mudstones, indicate that an ocean shoreline persisted in the area of the Grand Canyon until at least 1.1 billion years ago. Overlying these formations, known collectively as the Grand Canyon Supergroup, is a thick layer of Cardenas Lava, the remnants of the massive eruptions that occurred about a billion years ago as the great tectonic plates came together to form a single landmass known as Rodinia, a supercontinent which persisted for roughly 250 million years.

Then, as first Antarctica and then Australia drifted away, the western sea, the ancestor of the Pacific Ocean, began to expand. On land the cracking of the Earth's crust created massive faults that ran as crystalline fissures across the horizons. Ground that collapsed on the downside of the faults was less exposed than that uplifted to the sun. The forces of erosion wore these latter formations down to the bone, eliminating

Above: *Marble Canyon, 1872, by J. K. Hillers*
Left: *An open stretch of river near Unkar Rapid*

THE FINEST WORKERS IN STONE ARE NOT COPPER OR
STEEL TOOLS, BUT THE GENTLE TOUCHES OF AIR AND
WATER WORKING AT THEIR LEISURE WITH A LIBERAL
ALLOWANCE OF TIME.

—HENRY DAVID THOREAU,
A WEEK ON THE CONCORD AND MERRIMACK RIVERS, 1873

them altogether in vast reaches of the landscape. Thus today in certain parts of the Grand Canyon, remnants of the Supergroup are readily seen and define the stratigraphy. But in other stretches along the river, where by strict chronology such formations ought to be seen, they are completely absent, and a later Paleozoic deposit, the Tapeats Sandstone, rests as a blanket directly upon the Precambrian rocks, the Vishnu Schist, and Zoroaster Granite. In such places two adjacent layers of stone differ in age by as much as 1.2 billion years. This is what is known as the Great Unconformity. The rocks of the layered landscape that might speak of untold geological mysteries are simply gone, completely eroded and lost to time. If Powell's canyon is a library, and the rocks a record of a life, then half the pages of the diary have been torn asunder, leaving the reader struggling to understand the power and meaning of the slow corrosion of time.

The Paleozoic era, which began some 545 million years ago, marked a tranquil time in the history of the land that would birth the Grand Canyon. With the breakup of the Rodinia supercontinent, the region lay on a continental plate, far from tectonic activity. Erosion had left in its wake a flat lowland plain, which over time was swept by the ebb and flow of the Paleozoic seas. The crystalline dust and quartz sands of the ancient beaches compressed to form the Tapeats Sandstone. Mud and clay silts carried further from the shore settled into deeper waters, deposits that became the Bright Angel Shales. Further out to sea, calcite, crystallized from the salt water or derived from the exoskeletons of newly evolved multicellular organisms, precipitated to form a sedimentary layer, which, once compressed by weight and time, became the Muav Limestone. These formations, collectively known as the Tonto Group, span some 200 million years, during which time the deposits shifted as the ocean moved east, causing what had been geographically separated depositions to stack one atop the other, such that the Bright Angel Shale is seen today to lie over the Tapeats Sandstone, with the Muav Limestone forming a blanket above the shale.

Above the Tonto Group, there is another gap in time, for nowhere in the Grand Canyon is there evidence of the Ordovician or Silurian eras, a period of 130 million years that saw the birth of the flowering plants and the mass extinction of some 60 percent of marine life. In the west of the Canyon, Temple Butte Limestone, deposited during the late Devonian, the great age of fishes, lies above the Muav Limestone. But to the east this formation is absent and in its place is a layer deposited much later, some 350 million years ago, when oceans rose to cover virtually all of North America and an explosion of new life brought wild diversity to the seas, the corals and bivalves, gastropods, brachiopods, crinoids, bryozoans, and all the ancient shell-bearing marine organisms that etch to this day the shadows of extinct fossil life in the imposing Redwall Limestone cliffs that dominate the Canyon.

Then as the seas finally receded, leaving the limestone to crack and sink in the sun, the red sediments of the Supai Group accumulated for 25 million years, a time when the continent straddled the tropics and great glacial sheets reached north from the southern pole. When these in turn retreated, the land was flooded by sediments brought down from the slopes of the emergent mountains, ancestors of the Rockies. Reaching the flat plains, these rivers joined into a single somnambulant stream from which fell the muddy silts that became the Hermit Formation. These rivers of silt flowed across the region of the Grand Canyon for 10 million years, but then they disappeared, and a period of intense erosion began. Huge cracks appeared in the ground, and by 270 million years ago the region had become a formidable desert as vast as the Sahara, with dunes a thousand feet high. These sand dunes, which reached north as far as present day Montana, are still seen in the sheer cliffs of Coconino Sandstone.

Inevitably the oceans returned and after 5 million years of desert winds the seas swept over the land. The air, however, remained dry, the sun so hot that enormous volumes of saltwater evaporated by the shores and above the tidal flats, leaving thick deposits of salt and gypsum, which show up today in the Toroweap Formation. The sea continued to rise, and by 260 million years ago all of what is now Arizona was under water, and once again the ocean floor was littered with the deathly remains of sponges and bivalves, corals and gastropods, a deposit that in time yielded the capstone of Powell's stratigraphic profile, the Kaibab Limestone of the Canyon rim. Thus by 255 million years ago, the rocks of the modern Grand Canyon were aligned. But they were hardly in place, for they lay not as they do today at seven thousand to nine thousand feet, but rather at sea level, and there was as yet no river to bring their wonders to light.

The primordial continents, the great tectonic plates of Rodinia, having moved apart 750 million years ago, had, after millions of years, again coalesced, forming the new super continent of Pangea. When Pangea in turn broke up during the Triassic, some 250 million years ago, western North America was convulsed with cataclysmic volcanic activity that brought into being entire mountain ranges. These of course inevitably eroded, and sediments thousands of feet thick accumulated in the basin of the Grand Canyon, compressing the organic and inorganic materials of the Kaibab depositions into limestone.

As Pangea continued to separate into continents, North America moved westward. Its continental plate slipped over the oceanic crust of the Pacific, forging a chain of tremendous volcanoes from Mexico to Canada even as massive forces conspired to lift up the southern Rockies and the entire Colorado Plateau. What had been the swamps of a coastal plain became a high mountainous plateau, with only the underlying coal seams to recall the exotic forests of seed ferns, cycads, and giant horsetails that had darkened the shores. Exposed to intense winds and storms of the high reaches of a continent, the Mesozoic deposits eroded away, taking with them the traces of dinosaurs, and exposing the underlying Kaibab Limestone to the sun.

Still there was no Colorado River. Some 45 million years ago the Colorado Plateau might have resembled contemporary Tibet, a high basin surrounded by rings of mountains, with all streams running down to a series of enormous shallow lakes that ebbed and flowed with the seasonal snowmelt. Where the Grand Canyon is today, the rivers ran to the northeast to a lake, the remnants of which are the sedimentary spires of Bryce Canyon National Park. The headwaters of the Colorado were forged relatively early, perhaps as long ago as 45 million years. But the present course of the river was not established until a mere 5 million years ago. How this occurred is uncertain, but the prevalent theory suggests that what became the Colorado flowed through Marble Canyon but then turned south, away from the Grand Canyon and up the drainage of what is today the Little Colorado. Near the present area of Lake Mead a stream known as the Hualapai Drainage ran from a steep escarpment all the way west to the Gulf of California. The source of that river eroded, carving its way up and into what became the Grand Canyon, until eventually it breached the last divide separating it from the upper Colorado, thus forging a single path to the sea.

There remained but a single act to the drama. Seismic eruptions beginning around 9 million years ago and left some eight hundred volcanoes scattered across the plateau south of the Canyon. San Francisco Mountain, dominating the southern horizon and sacred to the Havasupai, soared as high as sixteen thousand feet when first forged from magma. Eruptions along the north rim of the Canyon within the last 1.5 million years spilled molten rock into the Canyon, plugging it with massive natural dams, which backed up the river for hundreds of miles. Eventually this too eroded away and the river continued its abrasive flow to the sea, moving 170 million cubic yards of sand and silt every year before the construction of the modern dams, three times the amount of dirt excavated to create the Panama Canal. Yet over the course of a million years the slow erosive scouring deepened the river by a mere fifty feet. The metamorphic rocks of the Inner Gorge, the Vishnu Schist, and Zoroaster Granites, stones half the age of the Earth, do not yield readily even as the river itself reaches "down to the stillness of original time."

✸ WE ARE BORN OF WATER, A COCOON OF COMFORT IN A MOTHER'S WOMB. AS INFANTS OUR BODIES ARE ALMOST EXCLUSIVELY LIQUID. EVEN AS ADULTS ONLY A THIRD OF OUR PHYSICAL BEING HAS SOLIDITY. COMPRESS OUR BONES, LIGAMENTS AND MUSCLE SINEW, EXTRACT THE PLATELETS AND CELLS FROM OUR BLOOD, AND THE REST OF US, NEARLY TWO-THIRDS OF OUR WEIGHT, STRIPPED CLEAN AND RINSED, WOULD FLOW AS EASILY AS A RIVER TO THE SEA.

WITHOUT FOOD A BODY CAN LIVE FOR WEEKS. WITHOUT WATER, MERE DAYS. IN THE DESERT IN THE ABSENCE OF WATER, DELIRIUM COMES IN AN EVENING, AND BY MORNING ONE'S MOUTH IS OPEN TO THE WIND AND SAND, EVEN AS ONE'S EYES SINK INTO ANOTHER REALITY AND STRANGE CHANTS ECHO FROM THE LUNGS. ✸

THE GRAND CANYON, POWELL REMARKED, SUBLIME THOUGH IT WAS, DEMANDED PATIENCE AND EFFORT TO BE UNDERSTOOD. HIS PROTÉGÉ, GEOLOGIST CHARLES DUTTON, SAID THAT ONLY THE MOST careful intellectual engagement would render full the wonder of the chasm. These modest reflections were never far from my mind as we finally set out down the river, for however joyous the launch and frivolous the fun of being on the water, there is for everyone who embarks on the Colorado a tremulous sense of anticipation. This after all is the river of our imaginations. Too much has been said and written, too many lives transformed by the passage, for anyone to drift casually into the open embrace of the Canyon.

In a remarkable and unexpected way John Wesley Powell's spirit and shadow hovers over every descent. His book, like a lodestone, dominates the journey. The guides and crew, everyone familiar with the Canyon, recite his accomplishments with reverence, pointing out landmarks, recalling from memory passages from his journals, even as those of us new to the river struggle to make sense of what he achieved. We begin at Mile 0, Lees Ferry. Powell named landmarks by events and hazards of his journey, or by some poetic allusion to the inherent quality of a place: Bright Angel Creek, Separation Rapid, Marble Canyon. In 1923 a topographer with the Geological Survey, Claude Birdseye, retracing Powell's journey, brought the discipline and perspective of an engineer to the river. A bureaucratic compromise during the tangle of conflicts over water rights had arbitrarily designated Lees Ferry as the divide between the Upper and Lower Basin states. Numbers came to augment the lyrical language of Powell, and any feature overlooked by his original expedition was named simply for its distance below Lees Ferry.

A mile below the crossing the first slabs of Kaibab Limestone mark the slow descent into the beginnings of Marble Canyon. On river right the Vermilion Cliffs shine brick red in the morning light, and to the south and west extends the Moenkopi Formation, one of the few remnants of the Mesozoic to be seen along the river. A riffle runs fast along the flank of a low bluff, churning together the clear water of the Colorado with the muddy discharge of the Paria, a stream known to the Paiute as Elk Water. There are no rapids, though the outwash from the Paria forms a broad fan of boulders that squeezes the river toward the far shore. In 1965 two park rangers flipped their canoe in the riffle and one of them, Phillip Martin, aged twenty-seven, though wearing a life jacket, died of hypothermia. A strange fate, I thought as we drifted past the first signs of the Toroweap sedimentary rocks, dying of cold in a desert where daytime temperatures can reach 60°F even in the heart of the winter.

For all the drama of the Canyon and the intensity of its whitewater, there have been remarkably few fatalities on the river. Powell's expedition, of course, lost three men, but none to drowning. Until 1950 no more than one hundred people had run the river, and five years later this number had only increased to 186. In that time eleven would die. By 1970, roughly sixteen thousand people a year were heading downriver, a figure that by the end of the century would grow to well over twenty thousand. Of the hundreds of thousands in the modern era who have come to know the Inner Gorge from waterline, only twenty have perished in rafts or kayaks. Another thirty-five have drowned swimming from shore, but these include many who died intoxicated, and several who chose suicide. Statistically, riding a commercial raft the 226 miles down to Diamond Creek, passing through 160 rapids, fifty-seven of which are serious, as the river drops 2,200 feet and the Canyon walls soar overhead 6,000 feet to the skyline, is one of the safest avenues of transport in the country, far less hazardous than riding a bicycle through the streets of New York, or driving a car on the outer beltway of any American city.

But from the river it doesn't seem so safe, and this is what makes it great. On his first descent Powell smashed a hole in the side of the *Emma Dean* within hours of leaving Lees Ferry. At Mile 4 the first traces of Coconino Sandstone appear on river

left, and just beyond, below the arch of the Navajo Highway Bridge that soars 467 feet above the river, spanning the canyon, elements of Hermit Shale grow out of the shores, again on river left. Already the Canyon begins to take form, and along the banks of the river—in but a few miles—is displayed evidence of fifty million years of geological life. Powell saw all of this with trepidation. Recalling in his account the morning of August 5, 1869, as he passed beneath the site of what would become the Navajo Bridge, he wrote of a "feeling of anxiety [as] we enter a new canyon this morning. We have learned to observe closely the texture of the rock. In softer strata we have a quiet river, in harder we find rapids and falls. Below us are the limestones and hard sandstones, which we found in Cataract Canyon. This bodes toil and danger."

In fact it did not, for Powell had yet to understand the nature and character of the river. In most rivers, rapids form when water, over time, runs over a boundary between hard and soft stone, such that the latter erodes to create a drop that forms a waterfall, a chute, or a cataract, an unexpected descent that can shatter a canoe. In the canyonlands, by contrast, rapids are almost invariably formed as the result of debris flows that pour out of the lateral draws and tributaries of the main channel of the river. These are not trivial events. The land is a desert, the earth parched, and yet the monsoon rains of summer can spill inches over the ground in mere minutes, as much as a foot in a day, generating flash floods that tumble and roar to the lowest point on the landscape, which almost always is a river. Thus in mere minutes tons of debris can wash down a draw at formidable speeds of as much as fifty miles per hour, creating an irresistible wall of dirt and stone that flushes into the channel and transforms the nature of the river. Though perhaps difficult to comprehend, the laws of physics suggest that the size of the stones a flash flood can move is directly proportional to the square of the velocity of the water. If a stream's velocity quadruples due to the rush of rain, the size of rock it can carry multiplies sixteenfold. On December 4, 1966, fourteen inches of rain fell overnight and a single surge at Mile 99 in the Canyon carried hundreds of tons of debris into a modest rift in the river, washing away Anasazi ruins that had stood since the twelfth century, and transforming a minor rapid into one of the most formidable hazards on the Colorado, the rapids of Crystal Creek.

One begins to understand the meaning of water and the power of hydraulics at the first of the serious hazards, Badger Creek Rapid, a fifteen-foot drop formed at Mile 8 by stones and debris flung out by Badger Creek on river right and Jackass Creek coming in from the left. There's an oily tongue of water to follow into the rapid, immense holes, boils, and haystack waves to avoid. The rapid is named for an animal shot nearby by the Mormon pioneer Jacob Hamblin. He cooked it up in river water and found, to his astonishment, that the water was so alkaline that the badger's fat turned to soap. The next day he continued south and west, passing by Ten Mile Rock, a great vertical slab struck like a dagger into the bed of the river and, coming upon another cataract with a sixteen-foot drop, named it Soap Creek. It was here that the next great stratigraphic formation of the Canyon emerged, the jagged, irregular walls of the Supai Sandstone. Hamblin, though he didn't know it, had stepped back in time 310 million years.

We paused for lunch on a sandbar just below Badger, slipped down the trough of Soap Creek in the early afternoon, and came upon the death site of Frank Brown at Mile 12, a modest riffle that today bears his name. Brown was a dreamer of the American West, a railway man who set out in 1889 to build a railroad down the Grand Canyon in order to bring Colorado coal to California. To realize his scheme, he hired an engineer named Robert Brewster Stanton. Fortunately for all of us, the Denver, Colorado Canyon and Pacific Railroad Company did not do well.

Ignoring Stanton's advice, Brown expedited the survey with five featherweight boats, unstable as logs and as delicate as forest leaves, easy to portage but so flimsy that two cracked in half on the train trip west. Stanton took one look at the gear assembled for the expedition and remarked very simply, "My heart sank within me." The parsimonious Brown refused to waste money on life jackets, though the technology had been proven. Stanton wanted a crew with experience. Brown treated the adventure as a lark. With all provisions for the expedition lashed on a single raft, they set out from Utah on the Green River in May of 1889. Reaching Marble Canyon on July 9, they portaged Badger and made camp just downriver, above Soap Creek rapids.

Brown awoke the following morning in a sweat. In a dream he had had a premonition of death, which that morning became realized. In a modest riffle, splattered with small harmless waves, his boat crossed an eddy line and suddenly capsized, casting Brown into a whirlpool just below Soap Creek. Weighted down with boots and heavy coat, with no life jacket, he did not have a chance. After a frantic search, the men despaired, and one of the crew, Peter Hansbrough, inscribed an epitaph on a nearby cliff. Six days later Hansbrough and a black servant named Henry Richards pushed out into the river. At the bottom of a rapid, known today as "25 Mile," the current forced them beneath an overhanging shelf. Shipping oars, they pushed off and just when they had cleared the obvious obstacles their boat flipped and both men drowned. For Stanton, a serious man, this was the tragic end of folly. He ordered the men to cache the equipment and supplies in a cave near Mile 30 on the river, and then on July 17, he abandoned the canyon, leading the men on foot overland up a side canyon toward the safety of the rim. As he glanced back at the river for a final time, he saw the corpse of Frank Brown floating out of view. The following year, when Stanton, properly equipped with cork life jackets, waterproof food bags, and steady vessels, returned to the survey, setting out from Lees Ferry on Christmas Eve of 1889, he would find Hansbrough's body, come to rest on a rock near Mile 43, parched by the sun and desiccated beyond recognition.

AT MILE 12 THE CANYON is already five hundred feet deep and the soaring bluffs reveal the distinct layers of Kaibab Limestone, the Toroweap Formation, and Coconino Sandstone, overlying a long slope of soft Hermit Shale that sweeps down to river's edge. Though the river drops only ten feet in a mile, the canyon deepens at five times that rate, for the walls on both sides incline upwards at a rate of forty feet per mile. As one floats down the river, the canyon rises on all sides, and within hours of Lees Ferry one enters a hidden world that only gets deeper and more mysterious with each passing moment. At Mile 13 the river cuts through the Supai Gorge, the Esplanade Sandstone cliffs that border the river on both sides precluding any possibility of scouting the whitewater. The first hazard, Sheer Wall Rapid at the mouth

of Tanner Wash, is a straightforward drop of nine feet over a shelf, but the next, House Rock, is far trickier. The river pushes left around the wash at the mouth of Rider Canyon and along the Supai ledges of a bluff before taking a turn to the right off the rocks. All the force of the water carries the raft toward river left and a huge standing wave followed immediately by a tremendous hole, either of which could readily flip a boat. I row Sheer Wall, but for House Rock I am delighted to hand the oars back to my guide, Shana Watahomigie, who effortlessly avoids the hazards.

Below House Rock Rapids we tie the rafts together and float for nearly two miles until reaching Boulder Narrows, where a single massive rock divides the river. These placid stretches are typical of a river that for the most part flows at a gentle pace of five or six miles per hour. The Colorado drops 2,200 feet in the Canyon, and only 10 percent of this occurs in the rapids, which are on average separated by a mile and a half. This still means that over the course of a two-week run there will be 160 moments of wild excitement where for short spurts the raft will plunge and buckle at speeds of up to thirty-five miles per hour, dropping as much as thirty feet in mere seconds. But most of the trip is a languid float in the sun, a time to reflect or to chat, and with a crew of more than forty the banter is constant. It is an impressive mob. The film crew works like a well-oiled machine. The young kayakers are among the top athletes in their sport, and every day execute moves that would give pause to a river otter. The guides are the very best, and they include George Wendt, a Canyon pioneer, and our trip leader, Regan Dale, a Californian by birth, though you would never know it. A veteran of some 250 trips down the river, Regan seems more like an Old Testament prophet. His skin is parched and freckled by the sun; his hair cropped short as if to balance the amplitude of his thick red beard. There is always a twinkle in his eye, yet few words are spoken, and this is the key to his authority. Men parsimonious with language, but active in deed, inspire confidence.

Regan's family had a printing press in Riverside, California, and in 1970 it fell to him to produce an early edition of one of the first authoritative guides to the Grand Canyon. That same year, by chance, a cousin who had been wounded in Vietnam had returned shattered by the war, and sought solace in the wild, a quest that had led him to the wilderness of the

YOU CANNOT GRASP THE SCOPE OF THE GRAND CANYON FROM THE RIM, HOWEVER YOU TRY. IT IS AT THE MEETING OF THE RIVER AND THE ROCK THAT THOSE LITTLE THINGS HAPPEN THAT MAKE THE LANDSCAPE HAVE MEANING AND SYMPATHETIC SCALE.

—PHILIP HYDE, PHOTOGRAPHER

Matkatamiba Canyon

Grand Canyon. After several months, he summoned Regan from the coast, and together they discovered the river. In time Regan would become a professional guide and draft into the adventure no fewer than thirteen family members, including his wife Ote, who ran our camps on shore, and his younger brother Tim, who without hesitation took responsibility for ferrying equipment worth many millions through every hazard.

Of all the guides the person who most intrigues me is Shana, and I find myself drawn to her boat. She says little, especially in the first days, not because she is shy, as some perceive, but because she is comfortable with silence. A single mother, aged thirty-four, Shana is Havasupai and one of the few Native American Park Rangers in Grand Canyon National Park. Known to her grandfather as Two Feathers, she grew up in a patch of pine on the South Rim of the Canyon at a time when Havasupai families had to seek permission from the government to leave the five-hundred-acre reserve that enclosed them in Cataract Creek Canyon. Her grandfather had a packing business, providing horses for tourists, and in the late 1960s he had dropped off a party and then run out of gas, only to be swept up in a bitter and unexpected November blizzard. He had tried to walk into the Canyon for shelter, and perished. Shana's family dealt with the tragedy by clinging all the more strongly to the traditional ways.

The Havasupai, "the people of the blue-green water," recognize themselves as descendants of the Anasazi, whom they call the Ancient Ones, and know that their people have lived in the depths of the western Grand Canyon and on the uplands of the South Rim for more than seven hundred years, growing crops in the canyon during the hot summer months, and retreating in the fall to higher ground to forage and hunt for antelope and sheep, mule deer and wild turkeys. Other interpretations suggest that they may be descendants of the Cohonina, a culture that first appeared in the plateau country south of the Canyon around AD 600. One legend maintains that the Pai came into existence west of the Canyon at Wikame, or Spirit Mountain, when two fraternal deities created humans from pieces of cane. They lived together until their children fought and the parents took sides, leading the Yavapai to break away as enemies, leaving the Havasupai and Hualapai on the rim of the Canyon as two peoples, closely related in language

and myth. Active trading occurred between the tribes, and with the other peoples of the Canyon: the Hopi and, to the west, the Mojave, and in time, the Navajo and Paiute. In exchange for shell and turquoise, the Havasupai offered tanned buckskin, dried agave, red ochre, and beautifully crafted baskets.

From these trading relations the Havasupai confirmed their vision of existence. The world was flat, and the sky a dome that came to meet the Earth around the margins of the horizons. The sky was as vast as the Earth was small, and the middle of the world was what are now called the San Francisco Peaks. There were four layers to the underworld, and four to the heavens where the sky people lived and shamans journeyed in dreams to confront their adversaries and influence the weather. The Havasupai recognized six cardinal directions, including the zenith and the nadir, the axis of existence. In the West was found a great sea and a land of a malevolent black spirit, who was countered by a benevolent white spirit of the East. After death the *kwidjati*, ghosts of the dead, could return to haunt the living, and thus the Havasupai practiced cremation and never again spoke the names of those who had passed on. To ward off ghosts and disease people wore hats with strips of porcupine skin with quills attached, or a sharp piece of obsidian hanging from the neck. They listened and watched for omens: a hooting owl forewarning of a death in a family, a porcupine in the dark—a harbinger of ill tidings. They healed with plants: juniper tea for diarrhea, willow sap for acne, a bit of salt for sore eyes. From Coyote they had learned the healing power of the sweat lodge, the sacred songs invented by Wolf, who took the first sweat. They believed that spirits dwelt in springs, and that the turquoise waters of Havasu Creek were as sacred as the river that formed the northern boundary of their tribal territory, the Colorado, which they considered to be the spine of the holy land of Ha'yitad, the homeland of their people.

The Havasupai first encountered Europeans in 1776 when a Spanish friar arrived and offered money to all those who vowed to convert to Christianity. Few did, and hostility marked all relations with the whites, culminating in open war in 1866–69. Cattle ranchers and miners encroaching from the south spurred the government to force the Havasupai from the Coconino Plateau into the narrow recesses of Havasu Creek and Cataract Canyon. In 1893 President Benjamin Harrison declared the Grand Canyon a forest preserve, a designation that

At the mouth of the Little Colorado River, by J. K. Hillers

Teddy Roosevelt, who famously described Native Americans as a pestilence to be removed from the plains, elevated to the status of National Monument, effectively imprisoning the Havasupai on their miniscule reservation. Missionaries, arriving in force in the late 1880s, criminalized the burning of the dead, the essential act of Havasupai funerary rites. In 1889 the Havasupai people joined with the Hualapai and the Paiute and embraced the Ghost Dance, the messianic dream of a new world, replenished with game and swept clean of all white people. The vision collapsed in the face of cavalry guns. The last Havasupai shaman died in 1960, twelve years before Shana's birth.

Despite this history Shana feels no antagonism toward the Anglo world. She knows, as she tells me, that the Pueblo peoples have lived in settled villages, with their languages and identities intact for 1,700 years. The Hopi village of Oraibi at Third Mesa has been continuously occupied for nearly 900 years. She reminds me that Pueblo Bonito at Chaco Canyon, built by the Anasazi over three hundred years beginning in AD 800, was at its height the largest apartment complex on Earth. The rituals of the Havasupai continue not for the sake of the outside world but as prayers for the survival of an enduring community.

The United States, by contrast, is not yet 250 years old. When we are all gone, when the industrial spasm is exhausted, the Havasupai will still be with their children in their gardens, planting, hoeing, weeding, and harvesting the crops of their ancestors. In the meantime, Shana celebrates the Colorado, the river sacred to her people, as the lone licensed Native American guide. She has only been working the river since 2006 and has rowed it perhaps a dozen times, but her quiet confidence at the oars and her deep understanding of its moods and power suggest that the river flowed through her blood long before she first rode it toward the sea.

WITH SHANA'S HELP I TRY to make sense of the river. I watch for debris flows coming in from lateral draws and drainages. Between the

CLOUDS ARE PLAYING IN THE CANYON TODAY. SOMETIMES
THEY ROLL DOWN IN GREAT MASSES, FILLING THE GORGE WITH
GLOOM; SOMETIMES THEY HANG ALOFT FROM WALL TO WALL
AND COVER THE CANYON WITH A ROOF OF IMPENDING STORM.

—JOHN WESLEY POWELL, AUGUST 13, 1869

Lightning strikes near Point Sublime

outlets of creeks and washes, where the river runs neatly past cliffs and soaring rock faces, the water is calm, a steady pulse slipping downstream at an easy pace, significantly faster than a somnambulant stream such as the Mississippi, but still a gentle, even sometimes tiresome, float. On the South Rim the lay of the land leads down and away from the canyon, and thus any streams flowing into the Colorado from the left bank originate within the canyon itself, and tend to be moderate in size. The North Bank tributaries, by contrast, descend from the highest heights of the canyon, with enormous forces that readily cascade boulders the size of cars and even buses into the channel of the river. Before the dams were built, the annual floods coming down the river had the power to wash away debris even of such a scale. Now the rapids build up, year by year, rock by rock, becoming ever greater challenges. There exists the distinct possibility that one day an aggregate blockage will become so severe as to eliminate any possibility of fair passage.

Around these stones and boulders the river roars, pouring over ledges and obstacles, creating terrifying holes as the water plunges to the depths and then spins back to the surface, rushing into the very void created by the hazards and the waves. The force of the Colorado running through these rock gardens into deeper waters spins whirlpools into being, many large enough to swallow a raft. Another dangerous dynamic occurs as the main thrust of the current runs wildly along the depths of the riverbed only to violently resurface as a boil of intense turbulence, a hydraulic surge that can threaten even a raft weighted down with a ton of gear and people. Eddy lines form below the rapids where the water by the shore reverses course and moves upstream, offering a respite from the relentless run of the river, though even these can be large enough to unsettle a raft. All of this is the natural way of water, moving down a slope. But on the Colorado the guides must watch for other signs. The volume of water brought to bear on the rocks and boulders of the rapids changes day to day, hour to hour. Every guide is aware, even in the depths of the Grand Canyon, of the well-being of Phoenix, for power demands fluctuate wildly. In 1977 there was a moment when the engineers deemed to release but 1,000 cubic feet per minute, three hundred times less than the flow of the original river at flood stage. In 1983, by contrast, they had no choice but to send

93,000 cubic feet per *second* down the canyon. Otherwise the Glen Canyon Dam might have ruptured. In riding the river, Shana tells me, your only loyalty is to the water at hand.

We camp for the first night just above North Canyon Rapid, allowing for a morning outing to the sunlit brilliance of an iconic slot canyon, where the light saturates the red rock of the Supai Formation, and folds of textured stone are reflected in a pool of perfectly still water. The following day we run a series of rapids known as the Roaring Twenties that carry us through the chasm of Marble Canyon, a slot that astonished Powell even as he ran—in a typical day, August 9, 1869—twenty-seven rapids in thirteen miles. "The walls of the canyon, 2,500 feet high," he wrote, "are of marble, of many beautiful colors, and often polished by the waves, or far up the sides where showers have washed the sands over the cliffs. At one place I have walked, for more than a mile, on a marble pavement all polished and fretted with strange devices, and embossed in a thousand fantastic patterns. Through a cleft in the wall the sun shines on this pavement, which gleams in iridescent beauty."

What Powell saw was not marble but rather his first glimpse of Redwall Limestone, the most dramatic and dominant rock feature in the Grand Canyon. Superficially, at least in color, it resembles the Navajo Sandstone of the Glen Canyon, but it is in fact a white stone, a sedimentary deposit, stained red over the eons by the seepage of iron oxides from the Hermit and Supai Formations that lie above it. It first appears at Indian Dick Rapid at Mile 23 as part of a low cliff on river left. Where exposed to the river and the abrasion of sediments, it really does look like polished marble—gray, not red—and sculpted into beautiful fluted forms, so exquisite that it only further saddens the spirit to recall that these formations that so beguiled Powell, and indeed everything we have seen since leaving Lees Ferry, would have been inundated had plans to build the Marble Canyon Dam not been stopped by the Sierra Club in the 1960s.

As we drifted into the beauty of the Redwall gorge, with the Canyon closing in even as the walls soared ever higher, with dark storm clouds gathering overhead, I thought of the late David Brower, the Archdruid as he was known, who had led the fight that saved the Canyon. I met him in 1971 when I was eighteen, a naïve college freshman. He was already a

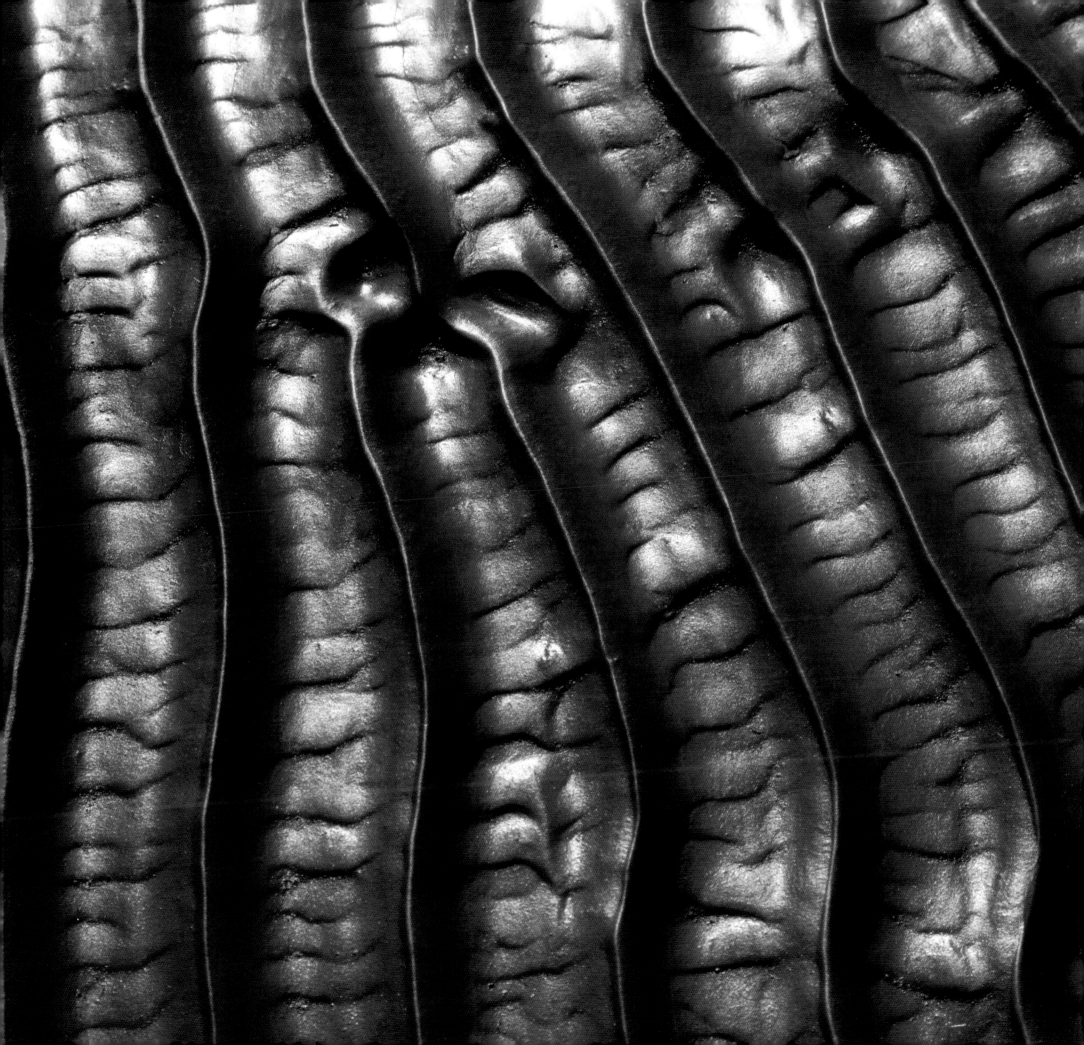

legend in the environmental community and I will always remember the day he bought me lunch, and with his wild eyes and dazzling smile all framed by that mad shock of white hair, told me never to forget that I had the ability to change the world. He was a great man, and he made me feel that I could make a difference, and had a moral obligation to do so. It is something of that spirit that Bobby and I hope to pass along to our daughters, Kick and Tara, as we make our way through the Canyon.

As the river turns east, the Redwall becomes ever more beautiful, horizontally banded in light and dark strips, a symphony of colors, with exquisite shapes upon which shafts of light move in and out of shadow. The walls appear, as Powell wrote, as if "set with a million brilliant gems. What can it mean? Every eye is engaged, every one wonders. On coming near, we find fountains bursting from the rock high overhead, and the spray in the sunshine forms the gems, which bedeck the wall. The rocks below the fountain are covered with mosses and ferns and many beautiful flowering plants. We name it Vasey's Paradise in honor of the botanist who traveled with us last year."

Amid the sands of the desert, Powell had found a lush oasis of delicate plants, mosses and maidenhairs, cardinal flowers and orchids, horsetails and redbud. Out of the limestone a third of the way up the cliff face gush two jets of fresh water, which land upon stones and run away into a series of small falls. We drink from the stream and are only later reminded that the water in hand originated as rain thousands of years before, settled upon stone and slowly seeped through more than a mile of porous rock, only to gather on the impermeable layer of Muav Limestone and spout forth from the bottom of the Canyon. At Vasey's Paradise, we drink the rain that had moistened the fields some ten thousand years before, at the very dawn of agriculture.

The storm had gathered and great sheets of rain swept over the canyon rim. At Mile 33 we stopped at Redwall Cavern, a vast and extraordinary chamber where the river has carved a deep and broad recess beneath the stone. In his published account, Powell captivated his readers by describing it as a theatre capable of sheltering an audience of fifty thousand.

A tenfold exaggeration, but the place is nevertheless astonishing, and an ideal spot to wait out a flash flood. I was sitting quietly at the far downriver end of the cavern, out of the rain but still able to see downstream where the Muav Limestone appears along the shoreline, providing a base for the Redwall Cliffs, which form a narrow aisle, truncated by yet another face that collapses the perspective to create one of the most dramatic vistas in the Canyon. Rain pounded down, dark thunderclouds filtered the sun, and an unworldly ochre glow infused the chasm. Suddenly I heard a rumbling of stone, a distant roar, that grew until, looking up, I saw fountains of water, thick with mud, explode as streams from up and down the rims of the canyon walls. A dozen dark waterfalls burst into life, sending tons of debris and slurry to the river below. These cascades grew into torrents, and the stones landed with explosive force, blasting the shores. Sloughs of debris and rocks built into small avalanches of mud and stone. Here I was witnessing the real forces that carved the Canyon. Not the gentle action of sand or wind on rock, but rather massive rivers of mud, thick and powerful, capable of dislodging anything in their path, sweeping boulders as heavy as 280 tons into the river, as in fact occurred in 1990. Erosion lost all meaning as a word. This was not Thoreau's gentle march of time. This was a force capable of reconfiguring a landscape and rewriting geological history in an afternoon.

O.A.R.S. guide Eve Barnett guides her raft through rough water

WE CAMPED THE SECOND NIGHT AMONG THE DEER AND REDBUD AT **BUCKS FARM CANYON,** AND SET OUT THE FOLLOWING MORNING TO FOLLOW THE RIVER AS IT TURNED sharply to the east to envelop the dramatic castle-like promontory of Point Hansbrough. The only moderate hazard was the President Harding Rapid, at Mile 44, where a massive rock blocks the channel and a recent slide on river right forced the rafts to go left, around the boulder through turbulence that can flip a boat. The first sign of Bright Angel Shale appeared on river left, about three miles below the Harding Rapid, and a mile or so after that we stopped on a long beach with the hope of finding the very spot where Jack Hillers had photographed a broad historic vista, looking back upriver. The goal was to ascertain through stereoscopic photography the degree to which the Canyon had changed in the more than a century since the Powell expedition.

In 1871 Powell had followed up the success of his initial descent of the river by pulling together a second expedition that, unlike the first, was manned by serious scientists and scholars. To document the journey he hired a photographer, E. O. Beaman. As both an art form and a means of documentation, photography had come into its own during the Civil War, when the battlefield images taken by Matthew Brady had so moved a nation. But the technology remained primitive, the equipment cumbersome, and the challenge of capturing images of landscape in as remote a place as the Grand Canyon was formidable. A large photograph required a large and fragile glass plate negative, which in turn implied a heavy camera mounted on a serious tripod. The collodion wet-plate negatives had to be processed in the field, which demanded huge quantities of chemicals and various supplies. Beaman brought along nearly a ton of gear, including several stereoscopic cameras. In a pre-film era, these were the photographs people wanted to see, two images taken in parallel such that

The ruins of the Anasazi Nankoweap Granary

The Anasazi ruins of Pueblo Bonito at Chaco Canyon

when viewed through an optical stereograph the landscape came alive in three dimensions. It was a technique, again coming out of the Civil War, that was used and celebrated by all the great photographers of the American West: T. H. Sullivan, William Henry Jackson, Eadweard Muybridge, and many others. Stereoscopic photography as much as any art form elevated the West in the American mind. Images of Monument Valley, Yosemite, and of course the Grand Canyon had captivated the American people, suggesting the existence of a land of dreams, with physical features of a scale that matched the boundless energy and ambitions of an immigrant nation soon to be the most productive and wealthy in the world.

Powell had hoped that his cousin Clem Powell would work with Beaman as an assistant, but when the young man proved to be both congenitally clumsy and lazy, he turned to a young boatman, Jack Hillers, whom he had recruited after a chance encounter in Salt Lake City. A fair-haired and blue-eyed German, an immigrant from Hanover, Hillers had fought for the Union during the war, and then at twenty-two had drifted west with the regular army, rising to the rank of sergeant before taking his discharge in 1870. Powell admired the young man's strength and work ethic, his willingness to lug heavy loads of gear without complaint, and Hillers, for his part, took an immediate interest in the craft of photography. In 1872 Powell and Beaman had a falling out, and Powell turned to another established photographer, James Fennemore, for the second leg of the expedition. Fennemore proved too feeble for the challenges of the Canyon and by midsummer, sick with fever, was forced to abandon the party. To his credit, he had trained Hillers to take his place. Thus began a collaboration and personal friendship between Powell and Jack Hillers that would last more than thirty years, with Hillers going on to become director of photography for both the Geological Survey and the Bureau of Ethnology, and clearly one of the seminal and most celebrated American photographers of the late nineteenth century. When Powell died in 1902, Hillers was one of those chosen to carry his coffin to the grave.

It was with some anticipation that we scoured the shore and the adjacent boulder garden, searching for the exact spot where Hillers had set up his tripod and camera. Bobby and I walked the beach, while Greg MacGillivray, our IMAX director, scrambled through the brush and rocks. After a

few minutes a shout of delight drew us away from the river to a large boulder where Greg was cradling in front of his eyes a print of the Hillers photograph even as he glanced up, comparing the image with the vista, a broad smile on his face. It was uncanny to be in the very footsteps of Jack Hillers, to know that Powell no doubt had been here as well. I could not help but see the view upriver through the prism not only of this single image, but through the eyes of the photographer himself. Hillers was perhaps most famous for his portraits of Native Americans, hundreds of which are catalogued at the Bureau of Ethnology. Unlike Edward Curtis, who viewed photography as a salvage operation, posing his subjects with the explicit intention of recording the last vestiges of what he viewed as a doomed world, Hillers's portraits, especially those taken at Powell's behest among the Uinkarets and Shivwits, were of men and women in contact with the white world essentially for the first time. In the portraits their eyes look directly at Hillers, even as his lens bears down on his subjects. Standing on a stone in the Canyon, discovering to our own delight that very little had changed, that the rocks and bluffs were the same, that even some trees were still alive that might have offered shade to Powell's men, I desperately wanted to know what Hillers's encounters had been like, what he had felt behind the lens, and more importantly, who really were these men and women whose faces he froze in time.

A SHORT DAY ON THE RIVER, a gentle float of ten miles along Redwall and Muav Limestone with Bright Angel Shale sloping down on both banks to the river, leads to Nankoweap Delta, a broad alluvial fan built up from the debris and rock flow coming out of a canyon of the same name, which issues from river right. Nankoweap is a Paiute name, first recorded by Powell, which describes a place where men fought and died, where raids occurred, and the ebb and flow of conflict bloodied the ground.

We made camp early just below the rapid, so that we would have time before dusk to position the IMAX camera a thousand feet above the river, at the head of a well-worn trail that rises steeply to an astonishing archaeological site, an Anasazi granary that clings like a swallow's nest to the underside of a cleft in the lower strata of the Redwall. Lugging a 350-pound camera, together with a hundred pounds of film, and perhaps twice that weight in miscellaneous gear, up such a slope was, to put it mildly, a bonding experience for the crew. But from the heights the vista was astonishing. To the east, the fan of the delta, crisscrossed with animal trails and the faint shadowy remains of ancient gardens, bends the river into an arc that runs along the base of a canyon wall that reaches to the skyline and the rim of the Canyon, located but half a mile away. To the west the rim is distant, at least seven miles as a raven flies. Looking downriver to the south, the Colorado runs away like an undulating serpent through a corridor of canyon walls. The granaries glow in the warm light. The stones and mortar set in place by human hands more than a thousand years ago fuse with the wall of the canyon and share its patina, a varnish laid down year by year, layer upon layer. There are some forty archaeological sites in Nankoweap Canyon, which date from AD 900 to 1100. Peering into one of the four open doors of the granary I looked in vain for traces of Indian rice or mesquite, perhaps a kernel of maize.

Anasazi is simply a word meaning the Ancient Ones, and refers to a culture whose history has merged with myth, such that all the living peoples associated with the Canyon—the Havasupai and Zuni, the Hopi and Hualapai—feel some connection, some mystic thread of memory that links them to this common if uncertain ancestral realm. Even the Paiute and the Navajo, who demonstrably have no historical link to the Anasazi, invoke some fraternity, some lineage. For the Anasazi are not just another tribe, another marker indicating the ebb and flow of political and ecological fortunes in the Canyon. They are the symbol and incarnate memory of a civilization that once dominated the vast reaches of the American Southwest.

We know this much to be true from the archaeological record. Around AD 400 there was an increasingly complex cultural realm in the region, a people we today rather clumsily refer to as the Basketmakers. They practiced agriculture, processing and grinding wild and domesticated seeds with *manos* and *metates*, and hunted with short spears, augmenting the range of their weapons with an *atlatl*, a spear-throwing device. Digging sticks were used to plant crops and to forage

for roots and tubers. The dead were buried, which implies they had notions of a spirit realm. Within a hundred years they had learned to fire pottery. Then, in a technological advance equivalent to the discovery of the wheel, they developed a fast-growing, high-yielding variety of maize, just as the climate turned in their favor. A moist regime set in. It became possible to produce food in surplus, which could be stored, and more importantly controlled, thus creating the prerequisite conditions for hierarchy and specialization, the hallmarks of civilization.

Over the next three hundred years the Anasazi came to live in concentrated settlements, the first villages and towns of the American Southwest. These centers over time became interconnected as nodes in a network of roads that linked people across an immense landscape into a single cultural and economic sphere. Chaco Canyon became the epicenter of the Anasazi world. The single complex of Pueblo Bonito, begun in AD 800, was under construction for over three hundred years. The walls stretch for 1,300 feet, embracing no fewer than seven hundred rooms clustered over five acres. The timbers of ponderosa pine used to support the roofs of the kivas, the circular ceremonial centers of the site, some of which are fifty-two feet in diameter and twelve feet deep, had to be transported dozens of miles across a harsh and forbidding desert landscape.

The entire complex was laid out with a master plan that aligned the lives of the living with the cosmic forces of the metaphysical realm. The movement of the heavens was captured in architecture, a geometry of sacred space that

At thirty-two thousand cubic feet per second, one thousand tons of water are moving through the river channel every second. If an average elephant weighs about five tons, this means that the flow of the river is equal to two hundred elephants coming by every second. A hole in the river may take up about a third of the channel so the hydraulic dynamics of that hole are about the same as sixty-seven elephants jumping up and down on your raft.

—Larry Stevens, quoted by Edward Dolnick, *Down the Great Unknown: John Wesley Powell's 1869 Journey of Discovery and Tragedy Through the Grand Canyon*, 2001

Left to Right: *Anthony Yap, Bram Role and Rita Riewerts crash through the rapids in a traditional dory*

Above: *First Granite Gorge from the film* Grand Canyon Adventure
Left: *First Granite Gorge, 1873, by J. K. Hillers*

allowed windows to focus the sunlight at the summer solstice, and oriented the site throughout the year with the rising and setting of the sun. Radiating from Pueblo Bonito was a network of roads that bridged arroyos and walked up bluffs on wooden staircases or in footsteps cut into the stone. Shrines and kivas marked the routes along which fine pottery and copper bells traveled from the Zapotec, oyster shells made their way from the Gulf of Mexico, macaw feathers came up from Vera Cruz, seashells arrived from Texas and California, and turquoise and banded pipestone came south from the lands east of the Canadian Rockies, along the same route that in time would lead the Navajo down the spine of a continent into the canyonlands of the American Southwest.

At its peak the Anasazi domain included perhaps twenty thousand farmsteads, four hundred miles of monumental roads and ceremonial avenues, and no fewer than 120 urban complexes, some of which rivaled Pueblo Bonito in scale. All was well. The drums and chants called forth the clouds, and the ancestral gods always answered with rains that came every year, replenishing the fields, bringing life to the seeds. The genius and spiritual insightfulness of the priests was confirmed. At the turn of the millennium, in the year 1000, the rains were better than ever, like something from a dream, and the people rejoiced. Then in AD 1090 something went wrong. The prayers that had been answered for untold generations fell upon deaf ears. When the rains failed, the soil, which had been worked for more than two centuries, turned to crust. The storerooms in the great pueblos emptied. With no rain, there was no corn, and once the stored seeds had been eaten there was nothing to plant. Drought brought in its wake starvation, and the people had no choice but to abandon their farms.

In their desperation, the priests and the political elite ordered the expansion of all construction, as if the act of building might appease the gods. Of course it failed to do so, and in the end those who survived drifted north, to wetter if less productive climes, to rekindle the elements of their lives. Some moved to the drainage of the San Juan, erecting fortified complexes such as Mesa Verde. Others found sanctuary in the Canyon, where the river ran and water could always be had. Thus in the shadow of the Redwall may be found today thousands of Anasazi sites, many as dramatic as the granaries of Nankoweap. Yet all of them echo the tragedy of Chaco Canyon,

for in the desert the climate is always fickle. Within a few generations, in the middle of the twelfth century, those who had settled and found respite in the Canyon were chased out by another, more severe, drought that rendered uninhabitable even the lands on the margins of the mighty Colorado. From that point on, the Canyon took on another resonance. No longer a place to live, it became a sacred destination, a point of return, where in fleeting moments all the First Nations might recall in ceremony the genius and monumental achievements of the Ancient Ones, those who had ruled the desert a thousand years before the tyranny of the European conquest.

WE SKIRT THE HOLE at Kwagunt Rapid, and continue down the ten miles of river that separate Nankoweap from the mouth of the Little Colorado. The tributary, the largest affluent to enter the main stem of the river in the Canyon, drains a large basin of some thirty-seven thousand square miles. Its flow is normally a radiant color, deep blue or aquamarine. Because of the rains and flash floods, it is today muddy and dark, thicker in sediments than the Colorado itself. This is how Powell found it on August 10, 1869, a foul stream "so filthy and muddy it fairly stank." One of his crew, Jack Sumner, described the Little Colorado as being "as disgusting a stream as there is on the continent," with little but slime and mud. It was, he wrote, "a miserably lonely place indeed, with no signs of life but lizards, bats, and scorpions. It seemed like the first gates of hell."

To the horror of his men, who hated the site and were anxious for home, Powell elected to hold up for several days. Much as he admired the dramatic view of Chuar Butte, which displayed in a single flank virtually the entire geological history of the Canyon, he had other things on his mind. This was the point of no return. Powell knew from the Hopi that a route led into the Canyon to the upper reaches of the Little Colorado. This was the last known overland escape from the canyon. Morale was at rock bottom. The men, as George Bradley would write in his journal, were "discontented and anxious." Powell took measure of the longitude and latitude to determine their position. His calculations revealed that they were as far south as Callville, Nevada, a modest Mormon settlement that would offer an escape from the Canyon. Every mile they traveled west brought them nearer to salvation. Given the condition of the men and the meager rations that remained, every bend in the river that led in any other direction would be a potentially fatal detour. On August 13, the day they once again set out on their journey, Powell scrawled a single notation in his field notebook: "Take Obs. Capt. climbed MT." Some years later, as he prepared his journals for publication, he would remember the day more lyrically.

"We are now ready to start our way down the Great Unknown. Our boats, tied to a common stake, are chafing each other, as they are tossed by the fretful river. They ride high and buoyant, for their loads are lighter than we could desire. We have but a month's rations remaining. The flour has been resifted through the mosquito-net sieve; the spoiled bacon has been dried, and the worst of it boiled; the few pounds of dried apples have been spread in the sun, and reshrunken to their normal bulk; the sugar has all melted and gone on its way down the river; but we have a large sack of coffee. The lighting of the boats has this advantage; they will ride the waves better, and we shall have but little to carry when we make a portage.

"We are three quarters of a mile in the depths of the earth, and the great river shrinks into insignificance, as it dashes its angry waves against the walls and cliffs, that rise to the world above; but they are puny ripples, and we but pigmies, running up and down the sands, or lost among the boulders.

"We have an unknown distance yet to run; an unknown river yet to explore. What falls there are, we know not; what rocks beset the channel, we know not; what walls rise over the water, we know not; Ah, well! We may conjecture many things. The men talk as cheerfully as ever; jests are bandied about freely this morning; but to me the cheer is somber and the jests are ghastly."

If the Little Colorado represented to Powell's men the very gates of hell, it was, by contrast, for the Hopi both the divine destination of the dead and the point of origin of all life. Descendants of the Kayenta Anasazi, the Hopi maintained that there was a time when animals and people lived together in free and open communication, with equal roles to play as denizens of the Earth. Then human vice shattered the social order and people had to move to another world. Thus the ancestors

of the Hopi were condemned to travel through the darkness of the inner Earth through a succession of realities until finally they emerged at Sipapu, a dome of rock by a travertine stream in the basin of what is today the Little Colorado. When the ancestors rose to the light, they saw footsteps and soon encountered Ma'saw, the guardian of earth and fire. Ma'saw allowed the people to stay, provided they vowed to act as stewards of the Earth. The Hopi agreed and the covenant was sealed with a gift from Ma'saw of corn and a digging stick. To this day much of Hopi ritual invokes this original promise. To plant corn is to grow food, but it is also to ensure the continued well-being of the entire Earth, which ultimately demands and implies the presence of water. Their prayers and rituals, their civic ceremonies, all pay homage to the rain, rivers, and clouds, and the sacred springs scattered throughout the canyons.

In time the Hopi clans carried the message of Ma'saw to every corner of the planet before returning to the canyonlands and finally settling at what is now known as Hopi Mesa, some seventy miles to the east of the Little Colorado. In death, their spirits return to Ma'saw and the place of origins, traveling through the cosmic navel of Sipapu to the underworld and thence to a new existence, returning to the land of the living not as human beings but as clouds that bring rain to the parched fields. In life this ultimate journey is anticipated and honored through sacred pilgrimage. Among the deities of the rocks of the Canyon is Salt Woman. Her shrine is a series of salt caves and overhangs close to the shore, just downriver from the mouth of the Little Colorado. Every Hopi male, as part of his initiation into manhood, must run the distance from Hopi Mesa, tracing the trajectory of the dead, marking the way with pictographs and prayer sticks decorated with the feathered markings of their clan. It is an arduous passage, and only those pure of heart and touched by deep humility will survive. To return alive, salt in hand, is to become a man. Today the caves are off-limits to visitors, as they should be. But as the rafts drift by, the low openings in the rock sparkle with mineralization, and faint colors identify still the marks of the ancient clans upon the stone walls of a canyon that remains a spiritual anchor of Hopi life.

To Zuni, the Earth is alive. The walls of Grand Canyon, the rocks, minerals and pigments there, and the water that flows between the walls of the Canyon are all alive. Like any other living being, the Earth can be harmed, injured, and hurt when it is cut, gouged, or in other ways mistreated. So, we believe that the Grand Canyon itself is alive and sacred. The minerals used for pigments, the native plants and animals mentioned in our prayers and religious narratives, and the water of the river and its tributaries are sacred to us and should be protected.

—Statement of the Zuni elders,
1994 annual meeting of the Western History Association,
Albuquerque, New Mexico

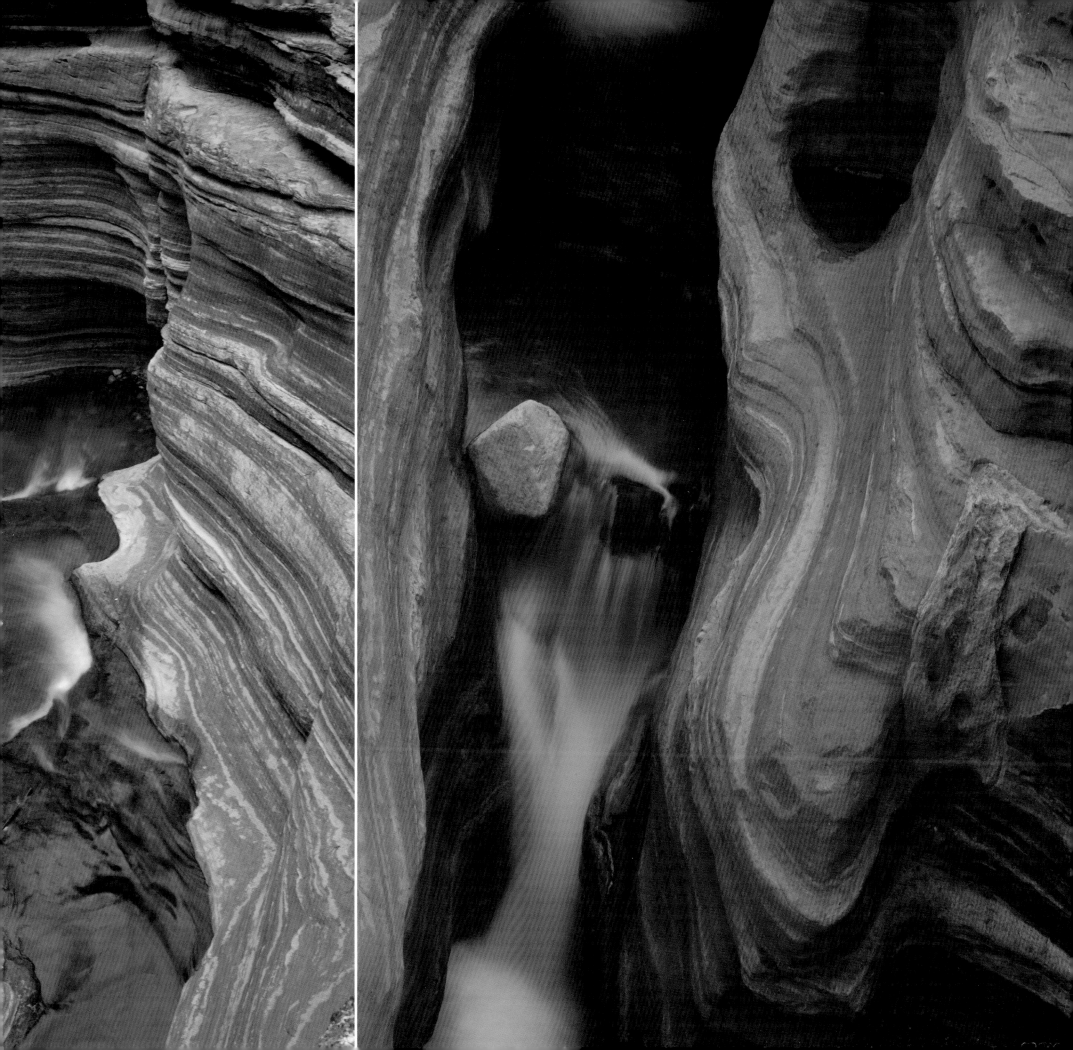

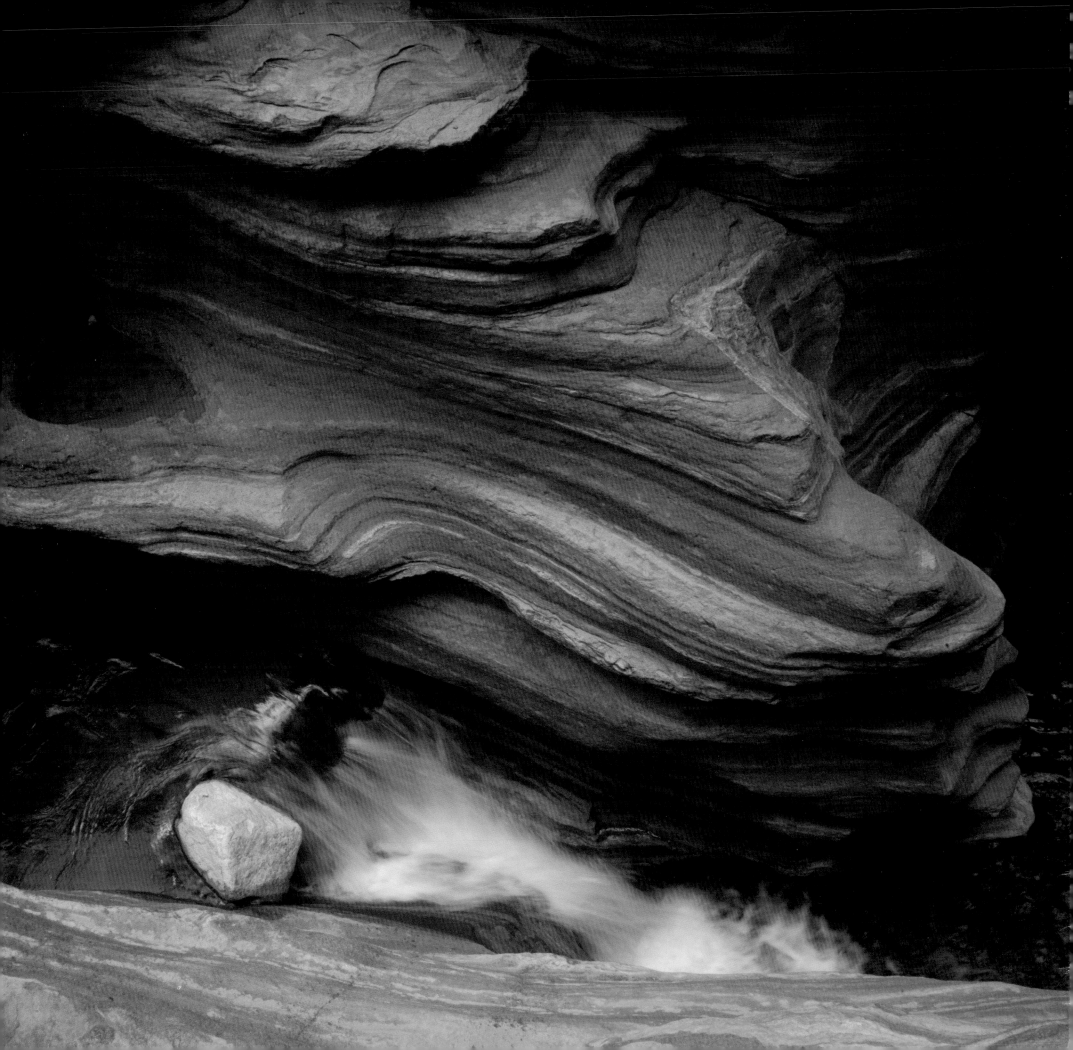

AFTER SPENDING MOST OF THE MORNING HAULING THE CAMERA AND GEAR DOWN FROM THE HEIGHTS AT NANKOWEAP, WE HAVE A SHORT DAY ON THE RIVER, DRIFTING THROUGH A TIGHT GORGE of Tapeats Sandstone to a camp at Carbon Creek. It is only our fourth day on the river, and yet already the tone of the trip has shifted from the initial excitement to a more settled pace. The film crew works seamlessly, anticipating and executing Greg's wishes. The guides are exemplary. Each evening they hit the shore and within minutes begin a sort of silent stalk for dinner, a seemingly effortless process that leaves none of the clients even aware that these men and women, having worked the oars all day, are now furiously preparing food for nearly fifty. No one has to be told what to do, and the easy banter among the kitchen crew has nothing to do with the dozens of tasks that must be accomplished if such a mob is to be fed. The food simply appears as if summoned into being. The kayakers for their part waste not a moment on shore. Oblivious to the cold, childlike in their excitement, they push against the current, leaping and spinning, disappearing into holes, surfing the crest of formidable haystacks until spinning out into an eddy. They hang in the water until the last moments of daylight fade from the sky.

Perhaps it is the simple pattern of the days that provokes this subtle shift of mood and consciousness. On the river you have no choice but to live in the moment, hour to hour. Time drifts away altogether and before you know it you have forgotten what day it is and don't even remember to care. Everyone slows down, sheds cares, even thoughts of anything but this place, this flowing river, its history, its drama. The landscape, initially as unreal and incomprehensible as an abstract painting, is gradually revealed and people who but a few days before could not have distinguished sandstone from granite are speaking in informed awe of the purplish hue of Bright Angel Shale, the incomparable beauty of a Redwall bluff.

A mile downriver from Carbon Creek the Canyon opens

up dramatically as the river flows through Dox Sandstone, a soft formation laid down over a billion years ago and readily eroded over the eons. The South Rim looms far ahead on the skyline, as we slip over the rapids at Lava Canyon, with the sun golden on Comanche Point, soaring over the valley on river left. The one hazardous standing wave and the big hole at Tanner Rapid are readily avoided. From there, the river opens to a broad meander that moves lazily through a basin dominated by the wings of a giant amphitheater of stepped pyramids and cliffs soaring to eight thousand feet, and named for the planets and the gods, Venus and Jupiter, Rama Shrine, Apollo Temple, and Vishnu Temple.

The rapids at Unkar Creek at Mile 72 are more formidable, a seething cauldron of whitewater where the river drops twenty-five feet and sweeps into a high cliff of dark shale on river left. Rocks at the bottom of the rapid can tear a raft to shreds, and it's imperative to stay right, hugging the inside bend. On the right bank a sloping bench rises to a crown of land where scattered stonewalls indicate the site of an ancient Anasazi settlement. It seems an austere place, but in the year 1090 there would have been some forty families living here. There is a sacred kiva, and remnants of the house sites and the walls that once protected the gardens from erosion. Most likely the settlement was occupied in the winter months when the men could fish and hunt, and later sow perhaps two crops of corn, one to be harvested in the spring and a second in mid-June. The summer heat would have signaled a move to the North Rim where another crop might be planted, antelope and deer hunted, and pinyon nuts gathered through the fall. This seasonal round lasted for perhaps half a century until in 1140 a drought, so severe and persistent that the Colorado itself may have run dry, forced the people to flee the Canyon for good.

When Powell and his men left the mouth of the Little Colorado, they did so "with some eagerness and some anxiety, and some misgiving," he wrote. "We enter the cañon below, and are carried along by the swift water through walls which rise from its very edge." Almost immediately they hit a series of rapids, three of which they felt obliged to portage, lining their

A Peregrine falcon swoops in for the kill

boats along the shore. These most likely were Lava Canyon, Unkar, and Nevills, a sixteen-foot drop at Mile 75.5 named after Norm Nevills, who led the first commercial river trip down the canyon in 1938. Here the canyon has narrowed, and steep cliffs of Shinumo Quartzite enclose a river passage that will not open up and widen to a valley again for more than two hundred miles.

That night Powell camped at the head of a cataract that was, as Bradley recalled, "the worst rapid we have found today and the longest we have seen on the Colorado. The rocks are seen nearly all over it for half a mile or more—indeed the river runs through a vast pile of rocks." This was Hance, a thirty-foot drop where the water runs through a gnarly garden of massive stones spread clear across the river. Named for a solitary miner who in the 1880s dug asbestos from the grim flanks, hauling it to the rim on the backs of mules, Hance is among the most formidable rapids in the Canyon. Regan Dale, our expedition leader, ordered the rafts to shore on river right across from the mouth of Red Canyon. On both banks beautiful cliffs of red Shinumo Quartzite rose above rust-red slopes of Hakatai Shale. As we made our way up the shore past catclaw trees and mesquite to scout the rapid, Regan for the first time sounded earnest, and the very tenor of his voice leant gravity to the moment, drawing in every guide close to his side. Never before on the trip had I heard him speak in full sentences. It was a tough rapid, with huge waves, boils, and churning holes that could readily swallow a raft. He prescribed a zigzag course, which everyone committed to memory.

Marble Canyon, 1872, by J. K. Hillers

Hance turned out to be a great tumble of a ride, a pounding half-mile of haystacks and holes that spat us almost directly into the mouth of the Upper Granite Gorge, where the entire feel and mood of the Canyon is transformed. In place of rich strata of sedimentary rocks soaring to the sky, the Gorge is narrow, even claustrophobic, a V-shaped cleft a thousand feet deep which runs for nearly fifty miles with neither beach nor shoreline to relieve the eye. The ancient metamorphic rocks are twisted and tormented, as if tortured by the heat and pressure that transformed them 1.6 billion years ago. The Vishnu Schist is black as coal, convoluted as if molded by some primordial artist, and running through it are seams of pink Zoroaster Granite, sparkling with quartz and mica. The walls enclose the river, channeling every sound. The roar of the rapids echoes up and down the chasm.

Powell shuddered to behold the entry to the gorge, for he was certain that metamorphic rocks implied ledges straddling the river, creating impossible falls and cataracts from which there could be no retreat. He never knew what awaited him around a bend, and the fear of coming upon a lethal drop could never have been far from his mind. It was not a trivial concern. At Grand Falls on the Little Colorado, the river plummets 185 feet, a drop higher than that of Niagara. His journal entry of August 14, 1869 records his trepidation: "The gorge is black and narrow below, red and gray and flaring above …. Down in these grand, gloomy depths we glide, ever listening, for the mad waters keep up their roar; ever watching, ever peering ahead, for the narrow cañon is winding, and the river is closed in so that we can see but a few hundred yards, and what there may be below we know not."

Later that morning, as if to confirm Powell's fears, the expedition came upon the first rapid that truly horrified the men. It was, he wrote, "a perfect hell of waves." The cliffs rising directly from the shore eliminated any possibility of portaging or lining the boats, leaving no choice but to run it. "The narrow river," recalled one of his crew, "dropped smoothly and suddenly away, and then, beaten to a foam, plunged and boomed for a third of a mile. The boats rolled and pitched like a ship in a tornado." George Bradley added, "The waves were frightful beyond anything we have yet met and it seemed for a time that our chance to save the boats was very slim." Jack Sumner, who had fought for the Union during the war, had never in his life been more afraid. "I have been in a Calvary charge," he later wrote, "charged the batteries and stood by the guns to repel a charge. But never did my sand run so low. In fact it all ran out, but as I had to have some more grit, I borrowed it from the other boys." Powell and his men named the rapid Sockdolager, nineteenth-century slang for knockout punch. It was only the beginning of forty miles of formidable whitewater.

On our fifth night on the river we camped at a beach just below Sockdolager and above Grapevine. Powell chose to portage Grapevine, inching his boats up and over precipitous rocks, his men passing the night sleeping in the open, "tucked around the cliff like eve-swallows." We ran right down the middle of the slot and fell almost immediately upon a series of cataracts: 83 Mile, Zoroaster Rapid, 85 Mile, and finally Bright Angel, which left us on the shore at Phantom Ranch. There at

the Ranger Station we rendezvoused with a couple of new crew members, and dispatched one of the lads to escort our exposed film by mule train up the Bright Angel Trail, a well-trodden track that leads in nine miles to the South Rim.

Powell and his exhausted crew arrived here on August 15, 1869, and had no choice but to hold over for a few days. Their boats were shattered, and they had to find wood to carve new oars. The beauty of the place, the sparkling clear creek rushing out of the mouth of an exquisite red rock canyon beneath the shade of willows and cottonwood, meant nothing to his men. The temperature soared to 116°F. They had been on the river for eighty days. They were hungry, indeed slowly starving, with only ten days of meager rations and no notion whatsoever of how far they had still to travel to escape the canyon of their despair. Morale could not have been lower. Powell fought and argued with the men all that day, first with Dunn and later with Howell. Things were falling apart. "This part of the Canyon," Jack Sumner wrote, "is probably the worst hole in America, if not in the world. The gloomy black rocks drive all spirit out of a man. And the excessive drenching and hard work drive all strength out of him and leave him in a bad fix indeed. We had to move on or starve."

And so they embarked once again, as did we, heading down toward Horn Creek, a formidable run where the river drops twenty feet in a burst of massive waves. Powell reached it on August 17, 1869, in a miserable rainstorm. The men had no other clothes than what they wore. Hats were long gone. They had nothing to provide protection from either the rain or the relentless sun. "It is especially cold in the rain tonight," Powell wrote. "The little canvas we have is rotten and useless; the rubber ponchos have all been lost; we have not a blanket apiece. So we build a fire; but the rain, coming down in torrents, extinguishes it, and we sit up all night on the rocks, shivering, and are more exhausted by the night's discomfort than by the day's toil."

Unbeknownst to Powell, the serious rapids were only just beginning.

SIX DAYS ON, WE MADE CAMP just above Granite Falls. In the evening we sought out another of Jack Hillers's locations, which I photographed just before dusk. It was a view upstream, taken from a boulder garden surrounded by white sand dunes which swept perhaps a hundred feet in elevation above the Colorado, indicating just how high the river reached before the construction of the dams eliminated the spring floods. The force of such runoff could reconfigure a beach in an instant, yet the very stones that Hillers shot remained in place, surrounded by datura in full bloom, poppies, and evening primroses, the same ephemeral plants that appear as wispy shadows in his photographs.

Regan's wife, Ote, has a botanist's love of plants, and she later guided me through the dunes, pointing out her favorite species. Like everyone in the Canyon she refers to datura, a low bush with white trumpet-like flowers, always as "sacred datura," a name I find curious, as the plant is in fact the toxin of choice of criminals and black magicians throughout the world. Its tropane alkaloids are powerfully psychotropic, inducing a psychotic state of delirium, marked by visions of hellfire, a sensation of flight, amnesia, and ultimately death. Shamans only occasionally and with great trepidation resort to datura when all other medicinal and spiritual interventions have failed, with the hope that in touching the realm of madness unleashed by the drug they will achieve mystical revelation. The rain priests of the Zuni employed it to communicate with the spirits of the dead, while in Europe witches applied extracts of related species to the genitalia with broomsticks that they might soar to the nocturnal assemblies of demons, which existed only in their minds. Calling datura "sacred" implies a sweetness and benevolence that the plant, however beautiful its radiant blossoms, most definitely does not possess. A common cause of death among those under its influence is drowning as they attempt to slake the burning thirst invariably induced by the drug. It is not something one would want to take under any circumstances, but most especially not on the banks of a surging Colorado River.

In the morning we walked the length of the rapid, again on river left, scouting the best route of descent. The alluvial fan of Monument Creek spits out a boulder field that pushes the river hard against a low wall on the far bank, creating a cascade of massive waves that run directly toward a rock island several hundred feet downriver at the bottom of the rapid. The maelstrom of whitewater appears formidable. The challenge, Shana instructs me, is to enter just beyond the boulders, keeping the raft as far left as possible to avoid the ferocious water where the waves careening off the wall collide with those moving in the opposite direction.

With Shana in the bow, I took her place at the oars and pulled slowly into the current. Clinging to her advice like a limpet, I dropped the raft into the rapid and had a good run, a straight shot that flashed by in a heartbeat. It was the first significant rapid that I had rowed on the Colorado, and I was amazed by the power of the water. On many rivers, certainly most of those I had known in northern Canada, it is possible to "cheat" a rapid, using physical strength and leverage on the oars to pull away from a hazard or rectify a lapse in attention or judgment. A river as powerful as the Colorado, by contrast, is completely unforgiving. The waves stand still, defiantly awaiting the rafts. Eddy lines can be ten feet across, with the water moving upstream being a foot or more lower than the river, making it virtually impossible to break across the eddy fence to return to the current. Whirlpools are not simply hydraulic sinks; they are massive black holes that seem to spin to and from the very bottom of the river. Boils rise out of nowhere, surging in places several feet above the surface. It is simply impossible to push the Colorado. You can only dance with it, placing your raft on the proper line, and hope that you don't pop an oar or screw up your alignment to the waves as the water crashes over the bow, burying the boat, and the river carries you down.

The rapids of the Colorado, as I learned on my first full day on the oars, come at you relentlessly, as Powell, to his horror, discovered on August 10, 1869, when he and his crew confronted no fewer than thirty-five serious hazards in fourteen miles of river. The day before he had made four portages and run twenty-seven rapids in thirteen miles. A week later the *Emma Dean*, with Powell sitting aloft, flipped, flinging him and two of his crew into the river. Two days later, on August 21, they would face six horrendous rapids in seven miles, "a perfect hell," as Jack Sumner noted in his journal.

And so it is on this river. Just a mile below Granite, there is Hermit, a sequence of five huge standing waves, each larger than the last, such that from the crest of the fourth, the final one appears as a mountain separated by an impossible valley, a deep trough that can take as long as three seconds to descend into and rise out of, assuming, that is, that your raft makes it to

the crest and does not flip. Three seconds in whitewater such as this can feel like eternity.

Below Hermit is Boucher, a thirteen-foot drop in the shadow of Point Sublime, which soars six thousand feet above. A mile further down is Crystal, an easy run in Powell's day that in the winter of 1966 was transformed into one of the most difficult passages on the river by a massive debris flow out of the mouth of Crystal Creek on river right. The river flowing across the face of the alluvial fan pushes to the left bank, dragging any craft toward two massive and dangerous holes that flank the mouth of Slate Creek on the opposite shore. As Regan explains at the scout, it is imperative to stay to the right of these holes, a trajectory that sets you up perfectly to crash into a rock island, situated just below the rapid. Thus, in a chute that concentrates the entire Colorado and plunges the river down a twenty-five-foot drop, one must execute in the middle of the torrent a somewhat delicate move, pulling the raft away from the rock island toward river left as soon as the last hole is passed. Go left too soon and the hole will eat you. Wait a moment too long and your raft may be shredded on the island. Indecision is not an option. With Shana sitting quietly on the bow, I managed to avoid the hazards and make it through, but not before colliding with another raft, which followed perhaps

River guide Shana Watahomigie

Man always kills the things he loves, and so
we, the pioneers, have killed our wilderness.
Some say we had to. Be that as it may, I am glad
I shall never be young without wild country to
be young in. Of what avail are forty freedoms
without a blank spot on the map?

—Aldo Leopold, *A Sand County Almanac*, 1949

Champion kayaker Nikki Kelly

a bit too closely behind us. It was not a pretty sight, but no harm was done.

Throughout a long and exciting day the rapids piled up, one after the other. First came Tuna Creek, and then the Jewels, a series of cataracts beginning at Mile 100: Agate, Sapphire, Turquoise, Ruby, and Serpentine. I momentarily lost an oar in Sapphire, and the twelve-foot drop at Serpentine took me by surprise and nearly flung me out of the boat. The Jewels are said to be relatively easy, and they are, but a mistake in any rapid in the Grand Canyon can be dire. After running Bass and Shinumo in quick succession, I was delighted to pull into camp just below the seventeen-foot drop of the day's final rapid at Mile 110. I was by then tired, wet, and cold, as was Shana. But the day had been exhilarating. I later scribbled a few notes in my journal.

"I cannot describe, nor would have ever anticipated, such a sense of release, such fun, as all sense of time fades away, all worries and concerns. I have not felt so free, so unencumbered in years. So many journeys I've made in my time, so many places have I come to know. The Sahara and the Amazon, Nepal, Benin and Mali, Polynesia and Greenland, the Canadian Arctic and the Andes of Peru, that voyage from Fiji to New Guinea through Vanuatu and the Solomons, twice around the world, Egypt, Tanzania, India, North Africa … but always my life has followed. But here it disappears. This desert, these people, this river is all that exists. Today I rowed Granite, Hermit, Boucher, Crystal, Tuna, Agate, the Jewels—Sapphire, Turquoise, Emerald, Ruby, Serpentine—and all the time these wonderful young kayakers were moving in and out of the river like dancers on the waves. Tonight the entire shore is lined with friends, all laughing and talking, sleeping in the sand under the stars."

MANY OF THE ICONIC SITES on the river remained to be seen, many rapids to be discovered: the travertine boulders and pink granite of Elves Chasm, lush with maidenhair ferns, cardinal flowers, and columbine; and Blacktail Canyon where, stretching your arms wide, you can bridge the Great Unconformity, touching with one hand Tapeats Sandstone, laid down some 570 million years ago, while caressing with the other Vishnu Schist, the metamorphic rock of the Inner Gorge, forged over a billion years earlier at the very dawn of time. The waterfalls of Deer Creek and Havasu still awaited us, and in between we would encounter the stunningly beautiful Muav Limestone of Matkatamiba Canyon. The rapids would continue, with Shana running the most difficult, Hakatai and Waltenberg, Bedrock and Dubendorff. Along the river the ecology would gradually morph, with the plants of the Sonoran—catclaw, mesquite, brittlebush, and barrel cactus—gradually yielding to the creosote bush, ocotillo, cholla, and a myriad of other natural denizens of the Mojave. Black-throated swifts skimmed the rapids, and in the rain one lucky morning we would be blessed with an amazing sight of Peregrine falcons on the prowl, dipping and diving toward the water, swooping high only to fall instantly to the kill. Along each shore, with each passing day, as if to mock the park regulations that restricted all movement on land, we would see ever increasing numbers of desert bighorn, an animal sacred to the Havasupai, tromping down the draws, trampling vegetation, creating in a single passage game trails that one day men and women would follow.

But even as we continued downstream, camping at Pancho's Kitchen or just above the beautiful rock ledges of Sinyala Canyon where we spent our tenth night on the river, all of our thoughts were moving ahead in anticipation of Lava Falls, the single most challenging run on the river and by reputation one of the greatest rapids in North America. In two hundred yards, we had been told, the river drops some thirty-seven feet along a gradient said to be the fastest navigable water in the Western Hemisphere. The Smithsonian once reported a speed of one-hundred miles per hour, a wild exaggeration that said much about the reputation of the rapid. The National Park Service offers a more sober assessment of some twenty-five to thirty-five miles per hour, still a not insignificant rate of flow for a river.

Lava clearly had intimidated and confused Powell. The night before lining his boats through the falls, an ordeal that consumed much of a day, he expressed both delight and worry in his notes: "August 24, 1869. How anxious we are to make up our reckoning every time we stop, now that our diet is confined to plenty of coffee, a very little spoiled flour and a very few dried apples! It has come to be a race for dinner. Still we make such fine progress that all hands are in good cheer, but not a moment of daylight is lost."

We camped the night before our run at National Canyon and at dinner I mentioned to Regan that I'd like to have a go at the falls. He generously agreed. I then approached Greg, who with delight indicated that he very much looked forward to filming the run. It was only in the morning that I realized what this impulse of mine had conjured in his sparkling mind. Drifting along the beach just after first light, I found the crew already at work building a rigging system on the stern of a raft. Not content to shoot the scene simply from shore, Greg's plan was to send me down Lava with a million-dollar IMAX camera mounted to my raft! I laughed at the audacity, though I remained nervous. As I made my way toward the kitchen for breakfast I ran into one of the veteran guides peering downstream by the water. He was checking out what he called Oracle Rock. If the rock is covered in the morning, he told me, you run the slot at Lava down the middle. If the water doesn't touch the rock at all you must go right. If half the Oracle Rock is covered and half exposed, you have a choice, and this, he said, was the magic. From what I could see we would be going straight down the middle.

Thirteen miles separated our campsite at National Canyon from Lava Falls, and to be honest I cannot remember much of anything from that late morning float, save a growing surge of adrenalin, part excitement and part trepidation. I felt fear, and recognized it as a good thing. On the shore the red walls of the Gorge yielded to black slopes of lava. A mile above the cataract a huge basaltic rock appeared in the river channel, a great slab that rose some fifty feet out of the water like some ancient funerary monument. Powell had named it the Vulcan's Anvil on August 25, 1869, just as he approached the falls. On all sides he saw growing signs of the volcanic activity that had convulsed this part of the Canyon, long after the river had laid down its modern course. "Great quantities of lava are seen on either side," he wrote, "and then we come to an abrupt cataract. Just over the fall a cinder cone, or extinct volcano, stands on the very brink of the canyon. What a conflict of water and fire there must have been here! Just imagine a river of molten rock, running down into a river of melted snow. What a seething and boiling of the waters; what clouds of steam rolled into the heavens!"

Powell rightly guessed that all of this molten rock, pouring into the gorge from craters scattered on the distant rim three thousand feet above, would have, over time, choked and blocked the canyon. A million and a half years ago there were, in fact, as many as thirteen different natural dams in this part of the canyon, the largest more than 2,300 feet tall and eighty-four miles wide. Such a dam would have backed up the river well into Utah, creating a lake that would have readily drowned Lees Ferry and inundated all of Glen Canyon, more than two hundred miles upstream. Eventually, over some twenty thousand years, these natural plugs eroded away, leaving the river once again free to run to the sea. In comparison to these massive formations, the modern dams at Boulder and Glen Canyons are mere irritants, certain to be gone in a flicker of geological time. Inevitably, in the end the river will win.

⊬

THE FATE OF THE COLORADO and the Grand Canyon was the last thing on my mind as Regan led us up a dirt path through a thicket of tamarisk and across a steep slide that led to a promontory high above the river from which we could scout Lava Falls. For a good five minutes he simply watched, saying nothing. No one else spoke. Each guide took his or her own measure of the water, finding the line, anticipating the moves that would make the difference. The curious thing about running serious whitewater is that everything goes well until it goes wrong, and then it goes very wrong, very fast.

Perhaps because of my inexperience in the Canyon, or the fact that the rapid had loomed so large in my mind for so many days, or because from on high everything appears intelligible and diminished in scale, I felt oddly sanguine as I gazed down upon this legendary bit of whitewater. It was not the shelf of lava I had expected. It was simply another debris field kicked out by Prospect Canyon on the far bank of the river. I understood what I was seeing, and wasn't overly concerned until Regan began to speak. He indicated the point of entry, a tongue of water that plunged into the maelstrom, and a massive hole, impossible to avoid fully. One had to skirt it to the left and then immediately spin the boat to come perpendicular to an enormous V-wave that would, he promised with absolute certainty,

completely swamp the raft. Weighted down in an instant with at least a ton of water, you would then have to turn again to align the raft to a series of massive standing waves—any one of them capable of flipping a boat—that would spit you at tremendous velocity toward a massive black boulder and a turbulent dead end of stones and whitewater known to the guides as the Cheese Grater. Should you end up there, Regan cautioned, all that would matter would be your survival.

I clung to his every word as I made my way back to the rafts. Shana did her best to reassure me, and I was grateful for it. I asked her to direct me in any way she saw fit. She told me to relax, follow my own line, and all would be well. We took on one other passenger, a charismatic kayaker named Zak, whose sole duty was to get behind me to turn on the IMAX camera and leap back into position in the bow—without blocking my view—as we dropped into the rapid. Fully loaded, an IMAX camera has a thousand feet or three minutes of film, but Greg wanted to shoot this scene in slow-motion at forty-eight frames per second, which only gave us ninety seconds, adding another challenge to a run already dependent on timing.

At first the view from the water seemed utterly different, as if to mock the scout as no more than a desperate act of reassurance. But then, oddly, the two perspectives merged, and I recalled without thinking the rhythm of every river I had known. Zak, on my instructions, did his gymnastics, and Shana, without any instructions, somehow passed to me her quiet strength and confidence. I kept seeking her advice, and she kept telling me to follow my heart. All of this transpired in the breathless moments before we plunged into the rapid. In an instant, the full force of the cataract convulsed the raft. I pulled away from the entry hole, struggled to find the proper alignment to the V-wave, catapulted the raft over and through the remaining hazards, and finally, fully taken by the river, flew past the chaos of the Cheese Grater. In mere seconds the run was over. It had been easier than expected, largely because nothing had gone wrong. I mentioned my relief to Shana who simply smiled. Only when I attempted to pull toward shore to ride the eddy back up to the landing where the other rafts were tied did I realize that the river had left me utterly spent and exhausted. It was all I could do simply to get us to shore.

Later that night, as the entire crew assembled below the falls on a stony beach, I found my way to Regan to thank him

for having given me such an opportunity. I tried to explain a few things, share with him some of my thoughts. But, in the moment, words failed, and all I could manage was the offer of my hand, which he accepted in a firm grasp with a smile on his face. I told him that running Lava had meant a great deal to me. He simply nodded, as if language in such a place at such a moment had no purpose.

VIEWED FROM SPACE, the Grand Canyon appears as a jagged slash on a barren landscape, with a narrow filament of a river, flanked at either end by the engorged reservoirs of the Hoover and Glen Canyon dams. On the northern side of the Canyon are the dark forested heights of the Kaibab Plateau, and to the south, beyond the Coconino Plateau, are the San Francisco Peaks and the forested flanks of the Mogollon Rim. East of the Grand Canyon lie the kaleidoscopic sands of the Painted Desert. To the southwest the river runs away toward the clouds of the Gulf of California. In a vista encompassing thousands of square miles, the one thing that is not seen is any sign of cultivation. All the efforts of all the engineers, all the billions of dollars spent, have not turned the desert green. After a century of effort and the construction of thousands of dams, including 1,200 in California alone— 50,000 nationwide—along with miles of aqueducts and canals, the area brought into cultivation in the entire West is roughly the size of the state of Missouri, and most of this has been made possible through the exploitation of nonrenewable groundwater. The wild rivers have been sacrificed but the desert still rules the West.

Though he would go on to great fame as the director of both the Bureau of American Ethnology and the U.S. Geological Survey, becoming virtually a patron saint of the Bureau of Reclamation, which was founded in 1902, the year of his death, John Wesley Powell, to his immense credit, recognized the limitations of the arid lands. In 1893 he helped organize the First International Irrigation Congress, which brought to Los Angeles representatives from twenty states and territories and a dozen foreign nations. Among the audience were any number of wild-eyed schemers and developers, promoters all. When

Powell saw their slogan, the promise of "a million forty-acre farms," all to be carved from the public domain and irrigated with the waters of the West, he became furious. Scuttling his written speech, he strode to the podium and delivered a broadside of unvarnished truth that horrified and angered many in the hall.

"I have decided on the spur of the moment," he roared, "not to present the paper I have prepared; instead I shall tell you a few facts about the arid region. I wish to make clear to you there is not enough water to irrigate all the lands; there is not sufficient water to irrigate all the lands that could be irrigated, only a small portion can be irrigated. It is not right to speak about the area of the public domain in terms of acres that extend over the land but in terms of acres that can be supplied with water. Gentlemen, it may be unpleasant for me to give you these facts. I hesitated a good deal but finally concluded to do so. I tell you gentlemen you are piling up a heritage of conflict and litigation of water rights, for there is not sufficient water to supply the land."

If only more people had heeded his message. Today the reservoirs of both Lake Mead behind Hoover Dam and Lake Powell above Glen Canyon have been reduced by drought to between a third and a half of their normal capacity, and scientific models suggest that they may never be full again. Snow pack in the mountains is much reduced. Ice fields are melting. The volume of water coming down the Colorado is at its lowest ebb since measurements began at Lees Ferry eighty-five years ago. Throughout the Southwest and in the basin of the Colorado in particular, stream flows are expected to drop between 10 and 30 percent over the next decades. Long-term climate models suggest that the arid conditions of recent years may in fact be the new climatology of the region. The drought, in other words, may be here to stay. At present more water is exported from the 250,000-square-mile basin of the Colorado River than from any other river basin in the world. Thirty million people, and the economy of the entire American Southwest and Southern California, depend on the river.

The driest states in the country are the fastest growing. Each year demand for water and power increases, even as the climatic regime shifts and supplies drop to new lows. Calculations and agreements hammered out in the 1920s have lost all meaning and relevance. As Bradley Udall, an environmental engineer and head of the Western Water Assessment, told a Senate subcommittee in June of 2007, "As we move forward all water management actions based on 'normal' as defined by the twentieth century will increasingly turn out to be bad bets." Udall knows his science and his desert. His family has been around the Southwest for a very long time. His uncle, Stewart Udall, served as Secretary of the Interior under presidents Kennedy and Johnson, and was in part responsible for the legislation that saved the Grand Canyon. His great-great-grandfather was John D. Lee, who founded Lees Ferry and was killed for his part in the Mountain Meadows Massacre. Bradley Udall is of a new generation that will have no choice but to solve through conservation the water crisis bequeathed to it from the past. It will not be easy, but the only alternative, in the words of a prominent Western water official quoted anonymously in the *New York Times* on October 21, 2007, would be an apocalyptic collapse, in short, "an Armageddon."

Pat Keller

WHEN I LAST SAW SHANA, SHE SHARED A TRAGIC STORY THAT NEVERTHELESS FILLED ME WITH HOPE. HER COUSIN, WITH WHOM SHE HAD GROWN UP AS A SISTER, HAD suffered a terrible accident, falling to her death while observing and celebrating a lunar eclipse from the roof of a building in Reno. The family had immediately gone north to bring the body home for burial and, of equal importance to the Havasupai, to retrieve the personal effects so that they might be burned, thus eliminating any possibility that her spirit might be diverted from its sacred path and tempted to return to haunt the realm of the living. To the horror of Shana's family, the former mother-in-law, a white woman, for reasons only of spite, refused them access to the clothing and private possessions of the deceased. Only after an agonizing confrontation did Shana's brother manage to persuade the estranged in-laws to release the body.

By then it was eight days after her death, an appalling and even dangerous interval for the Havasupai. Tradition dictates that the family arrange for the funeral with utmost urgency and haste. Shana had arrived in the late afternoon and found friends and relatives gathered. The medicine man came moments later, and, with sacred feathers in hand, began to sing and pray, even as Shana, in her grief, flung herself upon the coffin. Other ritual singers arrived, all men, and for hours they sang as the women danced. There were speeches praising the character and kindness of the deceased, and invoking by name the memory of others who had passed on, thus ensuring that Shana's cousin would not feel alone as she journeyed to the Other World. Offerings were made, blankets to warm her body, an empty bottle of Jack Daniels. A medicine woman sprinkled petals of wild flowers on the casket to cleanse the corpse and honor its spirit. What few of her possessions were at hand were then destroyed, including even the boom box that had been playing a CD of her favorite songs as the family hosted and fed the assembled guests.

The following day the family gathered on sacred ground to lay her body down. Working in shifts, the men and boys with pickaxes and digging bars chipped away a grave eight feet deep in the Kaibab Limestone of the canyon rim. A storm gathered. The rain at first evaporated before reaching the ground. But then it came down hard, pounding the earth all around the burial site. When finally, convulsed in grief, the family moved to lower the casket into the stone, a bolt of lightning struck not a hundred feet from the grave. Nothing was said, and nobody flinched, as slowly Shana's cousin was laid to rest.

On the horizon sheets of distant rain continued to fall over the Canyon, but to the west there were shafts of light reaching down to the depths where the river flowed. The Havasupai will always be here, Shana told me, and the Grand Canyon will always have something to say as long as people have the hearts to listen.

Shana and her daughter Cree embrace with Havasu Falls in the background

M Y LAST IMAGE of the Grand Canyon recalls the soft, glowing colors of Havasu, the blue and turquoise hues of travertine stone, the green waters, and the yellow sunlight radiant in the spreading branches of a leafless tree. In the slim shadows stood Shana with her young daughter Cree, a perfect sprite of a girl, buoyant, inspired, independent, and free. For almost an hour she and Tara had been playing in the water, cold though it was. Cree had only known Tara for a day, yet some chord already existed between them. Shana and I watched laughing as Cree leapt into Tara's arms to avoid the cold, utterly confident in the grasp of a stranger. It was at this point, long past the dances and ceremonies, the prayers and the songs, that we both knew that this Canyon adventure had brought our families together, with bonds of memory and loyalty that would never be forgotten. In a bloodstained world, these are the moments that allow us all to hope.

Afterword

Greg MacGillivray

THE FOURTEEN DAYS I SPENT ON THE COLORADO RIVER MAKING A 3D IMAX THEATRE FILM IN THE GLORIOUS GRAND CANYON WITH BOBBY, WADE, SHANA, OUR FILM SPONSOR TEVA, AND THE REST OF OUR FILMMAKING crew will forever be one of the great highlights and joys of my forty-plus-year filmmaking career. Working under the deep blue Arizona sky amid the Canyon's red-rimmed walls with such a dedicated team of like-minded conservationists inspired me in profound ways. It wasn't an easy production, though, and *Grand Canyon Adventure: River at Risk* will likely remain one of my greatest filmmaking challenges ever.

I've been in love with the IMAX Theatre film format for more than three decades and have been fortunate enough to make thirty-four giant screen films. As the world's largest film format, IMAX Theatre films have the ability to reveal the beauty and wonder of the natural world with unparalleled clarity, brilliance, and superior image resolution. The IMAX Theatre camera uses 70mm frames that are 2 inches tall by 2 3/4 inches wide—ten times the size of standard 35mm film.

Once developed, these images are projected onto the world's largest screens (up to eighty feet tall) with the world's largest projectors (which are the size of a Volkswagen engine) in theatres equipped with six-channel surround sound and seats stacked at a steep angle so that each member of the audience can get an unobstructed view of the screen. The result is an immersive, visceral "you-are-there" experience unmatched by any other form of entertainment

As IMAX Theatre filmmakers, our mission is to seek out extraordinary locations where we can take our audiences on

real-life adventures they might never experience on their own. We look for ways to put the unwieldy IMAX Theatre camera in places it doesn't want to go and into situations that defy sound reason. We've taken an IMAX Theatre camera to the top of Mt. Everest and down the entire Nile River, skysurfing out of airplanes and 350 feet below the ocean's surface. But nothing really prepared us for taking the even more immense IMAX Theatre 3D camera down the Colorado River through some of the greatest whitewater in North America. As my longtime director of photography, Brad Ohlund, said after our shoot, "We used to think that filming with the regular IMAX Theatre camera was backbreaking, but now we see how bad it can really be!"

The physical and financial logistics of shooting IMAX 3D in the Grand Canyon are daunting. The camera alone weighs 350 pounds and has to be carried by at least four people using six-foot-long poles. My co-producer Mark Krenzien likens this process to hoisting and transporting a refrigerator. At this size, the camera is heavy enough to buckle a rubber raft in seconds without the proper rigging. And filming in IMAX 3D is incredibly expensive. In order to create the 3D effect, you have to shoot twice as much film as you would with a normal camera. Two reels of 70mm film are loaded into the camera at a time—one for your right eye and one for your left. For every second of 70mm film exposed, it costs about forty dollars. A ten-second slate costs four hundred dollars—enough to make any production accountant jittery.

Despite these challenges, we planned to take the IMAX Theatre 3D camera plus thousands of pounds of additional gear down a river known for its raging whitewater and located in one of America's most remote environments. Not even satellite phones work reliably in the Canyon, and the National Park Service doesn't allow anyone to fly into the Canyon or paddle upstream. If our equipment malfunctioned, we would have no way to replace

Left to Right: *Producer/Director Greg MacGillivray behind the Solido IMAX Theatre 3D camera*
(one of only three in the world) with Stereographer/Assistant Cameraman Doug Lavender

Approximately ten thousand pounds of filmmaking gear were needed for the forty-four-person expedition

it. We could just as easily have decided to shoot on the surface of the moon. Because of these constraints, no one had ever planned a film production in the Canyon on the level that we did, and probably for good reason. But I knew there was no better way to tell our story and that the imagery we would find in the Canyon would be breathtaking.

The hyper-three-dimensionality of the Grand Canyon makes it a spectacular visual environment for IMAX 3D. There are already three natural planes in the Canyon—the boats in the foreground, the river's edge as the middle ground, and the epic background of the Canyon's rim a mile away. And I knew the river's world-class whitewater rapids would look especially exhilarating in IMAX 3D. All the right elements were in place to create an IMAX 3D experience that would transport the audience to the world's most magnificent natural cathedral.

Getting permits from the National Park Service was our first major hurdle. Very few film crews have been allowed to film on the main portion of the river because of the Park Service's commitment to letting visitors experience the Canyon's beauty without distractions. As a longtime environmentalist, I support their protective attitude. After all, we were asking permission to send a forty-four-person expedition—comprised of our film crew, Teva's team of champion kayakers and various marketing executives, and more than a dozen seasoned river guides—down the river for two weeks. Our expedition would be the largest in the Canyon's recent history.

We spent months presenting our plan to the Park Service and assuring them we would leave no traces of our production behind. Our company policy has always been to leave each location we visit even more pristine than we found it. After weeks of waiting, we finally got the green light—with one condition. A Park Ranger would accompany us at all times.

This forced pairing ended up working in our favor. The few times we were told we couldn't film in a particular spot because of the impact our crew would have on the site, our Park Ranger, Diana Pennington, took us to an even better vantage point to get our shots. The Park Service was key to our success, and we are indebted to them. We feel pretty lucky, too. For years the Park Service has been planning to change its rules to lower the number of people allowed on each river expedition; these changes were enacted just months after our journey's end. Ours was probably the last major filmmaking expedition to go down the Canyon.

Coordinating a filmmaking expedition of this size would be a challenge under any circumstances, but add a whitewater river trip to the equation and things start to get especially interesting. Our plan was to bring two IMAX Theatre 3D cameras (only three exist in the world and each is valued at $1 million), just in case one malfunctioned or accidentally took a dive to the bottom of the Colorado River. In addition to the cameras, we needed approximately ten thousand pounds of gear and fifty-seven miles of film. To feed the crew, our river outfitter O.A.R.S.—one of the most experienced and best-organized outfitters on the river—packed thousands of pounds of food, including six hundred eggs, 150 pounds of potatoes, two hundred loaves of bread, eighty heads of lettuce, and 100 pounds of lunchmeat. We were a veritable armada of twelve rafts and wooden dories, laden with people, gear, and equipment.

The real challenge of the trip, though, was simply maneuvering the heavy IMAX Theatre 3D camera around the Canyon to get our shots. This became especially daunting when we decided to hike the camera up the steep trail leading to the Nankoweap Granary located one thousand feet up the canyon wall. Here, the first farmers on the river, the ancient Anasazi, stored their corn and grain in dry caves built into the cliff walls. What came of this climbing effort must have been the toughest IMAX Theatre 3D shot to capture in history. The precipitous trail that leads up to the granary is filled with switchbacks, boulders, sharp rocks, and loose gravel—a treacherous path under any circumstances. It took ten strong men three hours to transport the camera and to keep it level—four in the front and four in the back, with two relief carriers ready to step in. Bobby and Wade even insisted on

Assistant Cameramen Rob Walker and Jack Tankard film Tara Davis paddling, as Production Assistant Rob Atlett, champion kayaker Anthony Yap, and Producer Shaun MacGillivray (front to back) stand by for safety reasons

pitching in as camera-bearers. It's a miracle we didn't drop the camera or injure anyone, but the results of our efforts—a beautiful shot of the historic granary and stunning time-lapse footage of the clouds and night sky moving over the river—made it well worth the challenge.

The production wasn't without its close calls, though. One late afternoon, at Granite Rapid—one of the toughest rapids on the river—I decided I wanted to film the team going through the falls from the water's edge downriver. To hike the camera from the top of the falls into position down below would have taken six people at least two and a half hours. At that point in the day, we simply didn't have enough remaining daylight. One of our guides, Tim Dale, said he thought he could run the rapid with the 3D camera attached to his raft and eddy out just below the falls. If he didn't make it, we wouldn't get the shot, as the next stop was another two miles downriver. It was a huge gamble. We decided Tim would do whatever it took to get through the rapid, and then gun his engine—hoping it didn't flood and die (which often happens)—in order to make it into the eddy. We filmed Tim as he made his attempt, lining up along the shoreline to listen for his engine. For one tense moment, the engine seemed to stop, but Tim fought his way through the whitewater, landed safely in the eddy, and deposited the camera without even a scratch. We proceeded to film the team running Granite Rapid.

The biggest highlight for me personally was watching Wade run world-famous Lava Falls with the IMAX Theatre 3D camera strapped to his raft. Wade is an expert oarsman with years of experience, but even he was nervous about running the historic whitewater for the first time. It's one thing to run Lava, but it's another thing to run Lava with a million-dollar, 350-pound IMAX Theatre 3D camera strapped to your raft. We were all well aware of the stakes—if Wade didn't hit it just right and the raft flipped, the heavy camera would sink to the bottom. Naturally, given his great skill, Wade made it through just fine, and we got some of the best footage in the film.

Some shots did come at a price, though. In one case, we wanted to film a particular shot of the rapids with a 30mm fisheye lens, but didn't have waterproof protection for the glass. So we crashed through the rapids, got fantastic footage, and ended up with a nice $12,000 repair bill from IMAX Corporation. It was worth every penny.

Left to Right: *Doug Lavender, Greg MacGillivray behind camera, and Stereographer/Assistant Cameraman Justin Bergler*

Although we had a lot of long, hard days lugging heavy equipment around and waiting for just the right light, we had a tremendous amount of fun together. There was always a lot of laughter and even some singing. Everyone sounded great in the Grand Canyon. It was an experience I'll never forget, particularly because I was lucky to be sharing the journey with my wife and son, both working crew members. Our fourteen-day adventure allowed me to connect four important tributaries of my life—family, water, adventure, and conservation—and I am grateful to everyone who helped us along the way.

In the end, my hope is that our efforts will result in a truly transforming experience for our audiences—one that gets people thinking about water as a substance that is more precious than gold. I want people to walk out of the IMAX Theatre thinking about that bottle of Evian, that load of laundry, that daily shower. We have enough water on the planet for all of us, but we need to be smarter about how we use it, and take better care to conserve what we have. We can solve the water crisis if we all work together, but we need to start now.

Left to Right: *Producer Mark Krenzien, Shaun MacGillivray, Doug Lavender, Jack Tankard, Robert F. Kennedy, Jr., and Rob Walker hike the 350-pound IMAX Theatre 3D camera down from Nankoweap Granary*

Film Contributors

Grand Canyon Adventure: River at Risk is produced by MacGillivray Freeman Films and MacGillivray Freeman Films Educational Foundation, presented by Teva and proudly supported by Kohler Co., in association with Reynders, McVeigh Capital Management; Museum Film Network; and Waterkeeper Alliance with production support provided by O.A.R.S.

MACGILLIVRAY FREEMAN FILMS

MacGILLIVRAY FREEMAN FILMS

For more than forty years, MacGillivray Freeman Films—a talented and innovative team of specialists in the development, production, and distribution of giant screen experiential IMAX Theatre films—has studied and perfected the art of motion pictures entertainment. Founded by Greg MacGillivray and the late Jim Freeman, this award-winning film production company creates positive, enriching IMAX Theatre experiences as it explores new and more exciting ways to take audiences on unforgettable adventures. Among the company's more than thirty giant screen film credits are *Everest, Coral Reef Adventure, Hurricane on the Bayou, To Fly!* and two Academy Award®–nominated documentaries, *The Living Sea* and *Dolphins. Grand Canyon Adventure: River at Risk*—produced in association with the MacGillivray Freeman Films Educational Foundation—is the company's sixth film in its ten-film series addressing water and ocean conservation themes.

MacGILLIVRAY FREEMAN FILMS EDUCATIONAL FOUNDATION

This not-for-profit organization was established in 2004 by Greg and Barbara MacGillivray to produce and fund educational giant screen films and companion programming that promote greater awareness and preservation of our planet's environmental and cultural heritage. Under the helm of Foundation president Chris Palmer, the Foundation supported the development of water conservation-related materials for students and the general public to accompany the release of *Grand Canyon Adventure: River at Risk.*

TEVA

Providing positive contributions to the world in which we play is inherent in everything Teva stands for. *Teva* is a Hebrew word meaning "nature" and the hand logo is the Hopi symbol for "friendship" and "water." For over twenty years, Teva has led the way in performance-based innovations in footwear, the platforms which carry the athlete beyond the offices of the day-to-day and onto the rivers, trails, and canyons of the next adventure. Teva is proud to stand along with Waterkeeper Alliance and the partners of *Grand Canyon Adventure: River at Risk* in this effort to promote water conservation, giving us hope that change is possible.

KOHLER CO. **KOHLER**.

Throughout its nearly 135-year history, Kohler Co. has remained true to its founding vision of defining the frontiers of ideas, craftsmanship, and technology. Kohler strives to establish new levels of excellence within each industry and market it serves as it fulfills its mission of "improving the level of gracious living" for each person who is touched by its products and services. Through the efforts of extensive research and product development, Kohler seeks to offer the most choices in low-consumption products for both residential and commercial applications and further establish its industry leadership in offering high-performing plumbing products that save water. With its large portfolio of water-conserving toilet, urinal, and faucet technologies, Kohler is well-equipped to provide aggressive water saving solutions for both commercial and residential applications.

DAVE MATTHEWS BAND

Formed in Charlottesville, Virginia, Dave Matthews Band has sold a collective 35 million units since the 1994 release of its major label debut, *Under the Table and Dreaming.* With 15 million tickets sold, the band—comprised of Carter Beauford (drums), Stefan Lessard (bass), Dave Matthews (vocals, guitar), LeRoi Moore (saxophone), and Boyd Tinsley (violin)—is consistently one of the top draws on the concert circuit and has implemented a plan to offset 100 percent of the carbon dioxide emissions from its touring activities since 1991. Its 2002 Lick Global Warming campaign with Ben & Jerry's resulted in fans sending over seventy thousand letters to Congress on the issue and pledging to reduce more than two hundred million pounds of CO_2. Dave Matthews Band provides support to numerous organizations, including Reverb, Bonneville Environmental Foundation, Clean Virginia Waterways, Habitat for Humanity of New Orleans, Rivanna Conservation Society, and Virginia Save Our Streams.

REYNDERS, McVEIGH CAPITAL MANAGEMENT

Reynders, McVeigh Capital Management teaches its investors that capital committed to good causes— when invested wisely—can be recycled again and again to create profound social change. Few investments offer as much potential to produce positive educational outcomes as giant screen films. Most of the revenues that *Grand Canyon Adventure: River at Risk* generates in the marketplace will go to support leading cultural and educational institutions around the world that house giant screen theaters. The film will deliver a critical message about the world's dwindling freshwater resources directly to 15 to 20 million viewers (in sixteen languages), and additional millions will learn about water resource issues through formal curricula designed for school audiences, through interactive websites, and through additional media associated with the project. The reach is simply extraordinary.

MUSEUM FILM NETWORK

The Museum Film Network (MFN) is an international consortium of cultural institutions joined by the mission to ensure that high-quality, science-oriented motion pictures are produced for the community of cultural institutions with IMAX® and OMNIMAX® Theatres. It began with six members in 1985 and now has fifteen prestigious member institutions: eleven are in the United States, and four are international. The MFN theatres attract more

than five million visitors each year and have retained their strong involvement in film production and cooperative projects to advance both the technology and the educational impact of giant screen films. Its most recent projects have been investments and participation in *Greece: Secrets of the Past* and *Dinosaurs Alive!*

O.A.R.S.

In 1969, O.A.R.S. founder George Wendt pushed off onto the Colorado River as the first non-motorized rafting outfitter permitted to run the Grand Canyon. In the decades since, O.A.R.S. has set the gold standard for first-class rafting as well as environmentally and culturally responsible travel on over thirty-five rivers worldwide. From escorting congressional staffers, eco-celebrities, and politicians on the waterways of the Western U.S., to establishing a model business for ecotourism operators in Fiji, O.A.R.S. is professionally committed to the cultural and environmental well-being of the places they visit. Through partnerships with environmental organizations such as Grand Canyon Trust, Idaho Rivers United, The International Ecotourism Society, Leave No Trace, Native Energy Travel Offsets, and Waterkeeper Alliance, O.A.R.S. actively supports awareness, deeper appreciation, and preservation of rivers and wild places. Experience the rich tradition of conservation and adventure for yourself on your next vacation.

WATERKEEPER ALLIANCE

Waterkeeper Alliance connects and supports more than 160 local Riverkeeper, Baykeeper, Coastkeeper, and other Waterkeeper programs—citizen advocates who patrol and protect the rivers, lakes, bays, and shorelines in their communities. The Alliance

supports our members with legal, scientific, and policy expertise and takes their clean water campaigns to the national and international level. Waterkeeper Alliance is the most effective protector of clean water because we truly act locally and organize globally. *Join us.* Get involved in the fight to protect our waterways.

Visit waterkeeper.org to learn more about the Waterkeeper movement and take action.

MacGillivray Freeman Films

would also like to thank the following for providing outdoor gear and products for the *Grand Canyon Adventure: A River at Risk* river expedition:
Teva
ExOfficio,
Immersion Research,
Black Diamond Equipment Ltd.,
Smith Sport Optics, Inc.,
Confluence Watersports Company,
and Horny Toad.

We also thank the following for providing promotional support:
Outside Magazine
O.A.R.S.
Wyland Foundation
ExOfficio

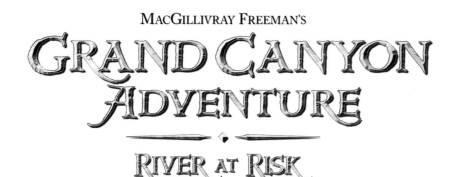

MacGillivray Freeman's

GRAND CANYON ADVENTURE

River at Risk

FILM CREDITS

THIS FILM IS PRESENTED BY TEVA
A Great Adventure Film®

PRODUCED AND DIRECTED BY
Greg MacGillivray

PRODUCED BY
MacGillivray Freeman Films Educational Foundation

PROUDLY SUPPORTED BY KOHLER
Kohler.com/SaveWater

IN ASSOCIATION WITH
Reynders, McVeigh Capital Management and
Museum Film Network

EXECUTIVE PRODUCERS
Chat Reynders
Chris Palmer

MUSIC AND SONGS BY
Dave Matthews Band

MUSIC SCORE COMPOSED AND ARRANGED BY
Steve Wood and Stefan Lessard

WRITTEN BY
Jack Stephens and Stephen Judson

NARRATED BY
Robert Redford

PRODUCED BY
Greg MacGillivray
Mark Krenzien
Shaun MacGillivray

DIRECTORS OF PHOTOGRAPHY
Brad Ohlund

AERIAL
Ron Goodman
    Spacecam Systems, Inc.

CINEMATOGRAPHERS
Greg MacGillivray
Jack Tankard

EDITED BY
Stephen Judson

ASSOCIATE EDITOR
Robert Walker

POST-PRODUCTION COORDINATOR
Matthew Muller

SENIOR PRODUCER
Harrison Smith

ASSOCIATE PRODUCER
Kathy Almon

LINE PRODUCERS
Sandra Stokes
Anne Marie Hammers

SCIENCE ADVISORY PANEL
Peter Gleick, Ph.D.
    The Pacific Institute, Oakland
Robert Ward, Ph.D.
    Professor Emeritus, CO State University
Theodore Melis, Ph.D.
    USGS, Grand Canyon Monitoring & Research Center
Janna Emmel
    MacGillivray Freeman Films Educational Foundation

IN PROMOTIONAL PARTNERSHIP WITH
Outside Magazine
O.A.R.S.
Wyland Foundation
ExOfficio

FEATURING
Wade Davis, Ph.D.
Tara Davis
Robert F. Kennedy, Jr.
Kathleen "Kick" Kennedy
Shana Watahomigie
Cree Watahomigie

CAST
Regan Dale
Dr. Kristin Kuckelman
    Crow Canyon Archaeological Center
Anthony Yap
Tanya Shuman
Nikki Kelly
Steve Fisher

ADDITIONAL NARRATION BY
Flo Di Re

1ST ASSISTANT CAMERAMEN
Robert WalKer
Jack Tankard

STEREOGRAPHER/ASSISTANT CAMERAMAN
Doug Lavender

2ND ASSISTANT CAMERAMAN
Justin Bergler

CAMERA LOADER
Joshua Kjorven

LOCATION RECORDISTS
Robert WalKer
Barbara MacGillivray

PRODUCTION COORDINATOR
Leonard Reynolds

GRIP
Jack Cruikshank

ART DIRECTION
Libby Woolems
Phil Clarke

LOCATION MANAGERS
PJ Connolly
Orville Sisco

WARDROBE
Liz Ferrin

STILL PHOTOGRAPHERS
Barbara MacGillivray
Chris Rainier

PRODUCTION ASSISTANTS
Rob Ablett
Michael Thompson
Zach Grant
Katie MacGillivray
Cindy Olson
Susan Wilson
Shakti Hu
Edward Benoit

HELICOPTERS
Southcoast Helicopters
    Cliff Fleming
Sundance Helicopters
    Tom Schaus

SPACECAM ASSISTANT
Vahagn Gharibyan

SALES AND MARKETING
Chip Bartlett
Alice Casbara-Leek
Nadine Ferdousi
Bob Harman
Mike Lutz

SPONSORSHIP
Patty Collins
Mary Jane Dodge
Lenka Spejchalova

PUBLIC RELATIONS
Lori Rick

ACCOUNTING
Jeff Horst
Jennifer Leininger
Pat McBurney
Victoria Stokes
Anne Tassinello

SOUND MIXING
Ken Teaney, C.A.S.
    Todd-AO Studios

SUPERVISING SOUND EDITOR
Andrew DeCristofaro, MPSE

SOUND DESIGNER
Tim Walston, MPSE
Michael Payne

ASSISTANT SOUND EDITOR
Patrick Cusack

FOLEY MIXER
Nerses Gezalyan

FOLEY ARTISTS
Jeffrey Wilhoit
James Moriana

RECORDIST
Robert Althoff
    Soundelux

VISUAL EFFECTS COORDINATOR
Matthew Muller

DIGITAL SPECIAL EFFECTS AND
END CREDITS PRODUCED BY
DKP 70mm Inc.
    Craig Rogers
    Steve Emerson

RESOURCE MANAGEMENT
Patricia Keighley

HIGH RESOLUTION DIGITAL
SCANNING & FILM RECORDING
DKP 70mm Inc.

NEGATIVE CUTTING
Nancy Paweski
German Nunez

OPENING TITLE SEQUENCE AND 3D
DIGITAL VISUAL EFFECTS PRODUCED BY
Alan G. Markowitz
    Visceral Image Productions

GIANT SCREEN DIGITAL EFFECTS TEAM
Lee "Bubbles" Nelson
Josh Mossotti
Andrea Caretta
Bill Leeman
Marios Kourasis
Miles Lauridsen
Mark Freund

John Campuzano
Jay Johnson
Jim O'Hagan

STEREO CONVERSION &
DIGITAL VISUAL EFFECTS
Sassoon Film Design

SUPERVISING PRODUCER
Tim Sassoon

VISUAL EFFECTS SUPERVISOR
Jeremy Nicolaides

LEAD COMPOSITOR
Colin Feist

COMPOSITORS
Jason Jue
Chie Yoshii
John Pierce
Rodrigo Armendariz

TRACK & MATCH MOVERS
Paul Haman
Lauren van Houten

DIGITAL ARTIST
Polet Haruntnian

EXECUTIVE PRODUCER
Chris "CB" Brown

COORDINATING PRODUCER
Jenn Bastian

EDITORIAL & DATA MANAGEMENT
Christopher Liu
Marc Van Der Nagel

POST PRODUCTION CONSULTANTS
David Keighley Productions 70mm Inc.
 Annie Toth
 Mark Humphrey
 Scott Price
 J. Todd Baillere
 Irving Barrios
 Kurt Schaefer
 Gerald Mantonya

FILMED EXCLUSIVELY ON
Kodak Motion Picture Film

COLOR BY
CFI-A Technicolor® Business

TIMED BY
Ron Wengler

ASSISTANT FILM EDITORS
Tim Amick
Hugh Sandys
Jason Stearns

SPECIAL THANKS TO:
WaterKeeper Alliance
Center for Global Environmental Education
Hamline University

Manuel Arango
Wilderness River
Glen Canyon National Recreation Area
Antelope Point Marina
Marianne Karraker
John grace
Steve Markle
Luke Thirkhill
Xanterra Parks & Resorts
Grand Canyon Railway
Grand Canyon Resort
Paul Fraser
Angel Martinez
Zohar Ziv
Pete Worley
Jill Ireland
Liz Ferrin
Adam Druckman
National Park Service
Diana Pennington
Chaco Culture National Historical Park
Hualapai Nation
Havasupai Nation
Navajo Nation
Kurt Nolte
Jack Sime
Steve Fisher
George Wendt
Steve Fleischli
Mary Beth Postman
Steve Abram
Northern Arizona University
USGS Grand Canyon

ADDITIONAL PRODUCT PROVIDED BY:
Teva
Immersion Research
Black Diamond Equipment
Smith Sport Optics, Inc.
Confluence Watersports
Horny Toad
Johnson Outdoors

STOCK FOOTAGE COURTESY OF:
4iS Four Eyes Ltd., Alexander Biner
Oribita Max, Jordi Llompart
Museum Film Network
Getty Images/Time & Life Collection
Real to Reel Productions, Inc.
Jeremy Rowe Vintage Photography
University of California, Riverside – Museum of Photography
John K. Hillers and United States Geological Survey – USGS

PRODUCED IN ASSOCIATION WITH
Museum Film Network
 American Museum of Natural History, New York
 Canadian Museum of Civilization, Hull
 Carnegie Science Center, Pittsburgh
 Denver Museum of Nature and Science
 Discovery Place, Charlotte
 Reuben H. Fleet Science Center, San Diego
 Louisville Science Center, Kentucky
 Maryland Science Center, Baltimore
 Museum of Science, Boston
 Museum of Science and Industry, Chicago
 National Museum of Natural Science, Taichung
 Omniversum, Den Haag
 The Orlando Science Center

Science Museum of Virginia, Richmond
Singapore Science Centre

AND IN ASSOCIATION WITH
Grand Canyon Adventure Film Network
 Imation IMAX Theatre, Apple Valley
 Fernbank Museum of Natural History, Atlanta
 Bob Bullock Texas State History Museum, Austin
 McWane Center, Birmingham
 Simons IMAX Theatre at New England Aquarium, Boston
 Ozarks Discovery Center, Branson
 Tennessee Aquarium, Chattanooga
 Navy Pier IMAX Theatre, Chicago
 Museum Center, Cincinnati
 Putnam Museum of History & Natural Science, Davenport
 Science Center of Iowa, Des Moines
 Detroit Science Center
 Gateway IMAX Theatre, Durban
 Telus World of Science Edmonton
 Museum of Discovery & Science, Ft. Lauderdale
 Moody Gardens, Galveston
 Whitaker Center for Science & the Arts, Harrisburg
 Houston Museum of Natural Science
 Kansas Cosmosphere, Hutchinson
 MAX Theatre at White River State Park, Indianapolis
 Science Spectrum, Lubbock
 Swiss Transport Museum, Luzern
 Milwaukee Public Museum
 Old Port of Montreal, Montreal, Science Centre
 The Maritime Aquarium, Norwalk
 Cinecitta, Nurnberg
 Omniplex Science Museum, Oklahoma
 The Franklin Institute, Philadelphia
 Arizona Science Center, Phoenix
 Oregon Museum of Science & Industry, Portland
 Menlyn Park IMAX Theatre, Pretoria
 Marbles Kids Museum, Raleigh
 Saskatchewan Science Center, Regina
 Esquire IMAX Theatre, Sacramento
 World Golf Hall of Fame, St. Augustine
 St. Louis Science Center
 Science Museum of Minnesota, St. Paul
 Clark Planetarium IMAX Theatre, Salt Lake City
 Pacific Science Center, Seattle
 Sci-Port Discovery Center, Shreveport
 Auto & Technik Museum, Sinsheim
 Science North, Sudbury
 Museum of Science & Industry, Tampa
 IMAX Theatre at Arizona Mills, Tempe
 Science World British Columbia, Vancouver
 CN IMAX Theatre, Vancouver
 IMAX Theatre at Palisades Center, West Nyack
 IMAX Theatre Winnipeg

FEATURING MUSIC AND SONGS BY
Dave Matthews Band
 Carter Beauford
 Stefan Lessard
 Dave Matthews
 LeRoi Moore
 Boyd Tinsley

LIE IN OUR GRAVES
Written by Dave Matthews Band
©1996 Carter Beauford, Boyd Tinsley, Stefan Lessard, LeRoi
Moore & David J. Matthews (ASCAP)

SPACE BETWEEN
Written by David J. Matthews & Glen Ballard
©2001 Colden Grey, Ltd. (ASCAP); & Universal-MCA Music
Publishing, A Division of Universal Studios, Inc.
on behalf of itself & Aerostation Corporation (ASCAP)

STAY OR LEAVE
Written by David J. Matthews
©2003 David J. Matthews (ASCAP)

MOTHER FATHER
Written by David J. Matthews & Glen Ballard
©2001 Colden Grey, Ltd. (ASCAP); & Universal-MCA Music
Publishing, A Division of Universal Studios, Inc.
on behalf of itself & Aerostation Corporation (ASCAP)

STEADY AS WE GO
Written by Dave Matthews Band & Mark Baston
©2005 Colden Grey, Ltd. (ASCAP); & Bat Future Music,
administered by Songs of Universal, Inc. (BMI)

TWO STEP
Written by David J. Matthews
©1996 David J. Matthews (ASCAP)

SPECIAL MUSICAL PERFORMANCES
Carter Beauford
Tim Reynolds
Greg Leisz – Steel Guitar
Richard Hardy – Flute
Mike Hamilton – Guitar

WITH SPECIAL THANKS TO
Bruce Flohr
Redlight Management

Worldwide rights administered by Colden Grey, Ltd.
(ASCAP) except as otherwise indicated.
Used by Permission.
International Copyright Secured.
All Rights Reserved.

PRODUCED AND DISTRIBUTED BY
MacGillivray Freeman Films
Laguna Beach, California

www.grandcanyonadventurefilm.com

Colophon

Earth Aware Editions

17 Paul Drive
San Rafael, CA 94903
800.688.2218
www.earthawareeditions.com

Publisher & Creative Director: Raoul Goff
Executive Directors: Peter Beren & Michael Madden
Art Director: Iain Morris
Designer: Barbara Genetin
Acquiring Editor: Jake Gerli
Editorial Associate: Mikayla Butchart
Production Managers: Lina S. Palma-Temena & Jonathan Mills
Prepress and Print Supervision: Noah Potkin
Traffic Manager: Donna Lee

Earth Aware Editions would like to thank Lori Rick, Mary Beth Postman, Lori Morash, Eddie Scher, George Wendt, Steve Markle, Mark Burstein, Heather Hutson, and Gabe Ely.

Library of Congress Cataloging-in-Publication Data available.

ISBN-978-1-60109-013-3

Palace Press International, in association with Roots of Peace, will plant two trees for each tree used in the manufacturing of this book. Roots of Peace is an internationally renowned humanitarian organization dedicated to eradicating landmines worldwide and converting war-torn lands into productive farms and wildlife habitats. Together, we will plant 2 million fruit and nut trees in Afghanistan and provide farmers there with the skills and support necessary for sustainable land use.

10 9 8 7 6 5 4 3 2 1

Printed in China by Palace Press International
www.palacepress.com

All photographs © 2008 Chris Rainier, with the exception of:
© 2008 MacDuff Everton: Jacket, Cover, pages 6–7, 49–50, 74–75, 80–81, 100–101
© 2008 MacGillivray Freeman Films: pages 13, 22 (second from left), 25, 36, 82–83, 123, 159, 163 (top)
© 2008 Wade Davis: pages 19, 22 (second from right), 44, 91, 116–119, 147, 154, 158, 162 (bottom)
© 2008 Jack Stephens: page 22 (far left)
© 2008 Michael Nichols: pages 32, 56–57, 66–67, 72–73, 88–89, 108–109, 148–149, 157
© 2008 Alan Kozlowski: pages 84–85, 124, 156
© 2008 James Kaiser: pages 41, 48, 51
© 2008 Wernher Kreutein: pages 59, 141
© 2008 Ben Horton: pages 112, 138–139
© 2008 Barbara MacGillivray: pages 22 (far right), 161, 163 (bottom)

Historical and stock photographs courtesy of:
Joseph Hillers: pages 35, 53, 64–65, 71, 77, 93, 106, 122, 142
NASA: page 90
USGS: pages 60, 61 (Christopher Taesali)